FRESH & TASTY

Low Fat Cookbook

BARNES
&NOBLE
BOOKS
NEW YORK

Copyright © 2002 by Richard Carroll

This edition published by Barnes & Noble, Inc.,
by arrangement with R&R Publications Marketing Pty. Ltd.

Publisher: Richard Carroll
Creative Director: Paul Sims
Production Manager: Anthony Carroll
Computer Graphics: Lucy Adams
Food Photography: Robert Monro, Warren Webb, Andrew Warn, William Meppem, Andrew Elton,
Quentin Bacon, Gary Smith, Per Ericson
Food Stylists: Ann Fayle, Susan Bell, Coty Hahn, Janet Lodge, Di Kirby
Recipe Development: Ellen Argyriou, Di Kirby, Janet Lodge
Proof Reader: Cindy Brown

Includes index
ISBN 0 7607 3353 8
EAN 9 780760 733530

First edition printed March 2002
Computer Typeset in Garamond, Times New Roman & Humanist

Printed in Singapore

Contents

Introduction

Eating too much fat is a major cause of heart disease and obesity. Eating too much saturated fat tends to raise blood cholesterol levels. High blood cholesterol is one of the major risk factors for heart disease. There are three types of fat in food: saturated, monounsaturated, and polyunsaturated. All fatty foods are actually a mixture of these three types. However, foods are classified according to the type of fat present in the largest amount.

Saturated fats
Tend to raise blood cholesterol levels. Foods high in saturated fat include fatty meats, full-cream dairy products, coconut, and the fats used for commercial deep-frying (ie. take-out foods, processed foods, commercial cakes, biscuits and pastries – palm oil is a saturated fat commonly used). If you have a high blood cholesterol level you should therefore try to cut down on these foods.

Trans fats
Are a small class of fats found in the fat of dairy products, some meats, commercial frying oils, and some margarine. Trans fats tend to raise blood cholesterol levels. They have now been removed from many margarines available today - look for a brand with less than 1% trans fats.

Polyunsaturated fats
Tend to help lower blood cholesterol levels. These fats come mostly from vegetable oils like grapeseed, safflower and corn oil, nuts, and many margarines.

A particular type of polyunsaturated fat called Omega-3 has been found to reduce coronary risk in other ways. These fats reduce the tendency of blood to clot, help lower blood triglyceride levels, and help protect the heart from arrhythmia (an irregular heart beat). Omega-3 fats are found in seeds and seed oils and in particular in fish. It is recommended that you eat fish at least two or three times a week.

Monounsaturated fats
Also help lower blood cholesterol levels. These fats come mostly from olive and canola oils and margarine as well as oils made from nuts such as peanut oil.

There is considerable debate about which type of fat is best. There are many factors to consider, but studies so far indicate that monounsaturated and polyunsaturated fats are equivalent in terms of their potential to reduce coronary risk. The most important aim should be to lower your saturated and trans fats intake. Both monounsaturated and polyunsaturated fats are better choices.

Remember all types of fats are equally fattening. If one of your goals is to lose weight, then you need to limit the total amount of all fat including these 'good' fats.

Another area of controversy is how much fat is acceptable, particularly if you are not overweight. Some experts state that we should limit all types of fats. Others argue that if the majority of fat eaten is unsaturated, then we can eat higher amounts of fat. The debate continues, but probably most of us need to think in terms of limiting our total fat intake so that about 25-30% of calories (kilojoules) come from fat.

This would be equivalent to:
- $1^1/_2$-$2^1/_2$ oz fat a day for most women and children
- 2-$3^1/_2$ oz fat a day for most men.

A healthy fat intake is based on your energy needs, your age and activity levels. Younger or very active people can eat more fat than those who are older or less active.

To lose weight, estimate how much fat you are eating currently and aim to eat less than this. You may need to aim for less than $1^1/_2$ oz a day. If you are underweight, or choose to eat more fat than this, then it is best to choose unsaturated fats, e.g. nuts, seeds, and avocado.

Tips for trimming fat

- Steer clear of fried takeaway foods – the type of fat/oil used is often palm oil (saturated fat).
- Choose cakes and biscuits that are low in fat and contain unsaturated fat. Home bake using unsaturated fat/oil, or commercial products that are either low-fat and/or the type of fat is clearly unsaturated (not "vegetable oil," which will commonly be palm oil).
- Choose healthy snacks, such as fresh fruit, dried fruit, bread sticks, and pretzels rather than potato crisps or corn chips. Nuts are healthy too, but go easy if you need to lose weight.
- Choose low-fat or reduced-fat dairy products: milk and yogurt with $^1/_{30}$ oz fat per $3^1/_2$ oz or less; cheese with $^1/_3$ oz fat per $3^1/_2$ oz or less; ice cream with $^1/_6$ oz fat per $3^1/_2$ oz or less.

- Choose lean cuts of meats and remove the skin from poultry. Go easy on your serving size. There is no need to avoid red meat – it is an excellent source of iron.
- Eat more fish, including canned varieties.
- Go easy on the amount of margarine you use on bread and toast – one level teaspoon per slice is ample. For a change, use avocado, cottage cheese, chutney, or mustard instead.
- Go easy on the amount of oil you use in cooking. Use low-fat cooking methods such as grilling, microwaving, boiling, steaming, and barbecuing, and use nonstick pans.
- Remember fruit, vegetables, breads, and cereals are mostly very low-fat foods and when they do contain fat, it is the unsaturated type.

Soups, Starters, and Salads

Long gone are the days of torturing yourself with
skimpy salads and bland soups in your quest for
healthy living. We have gone to great lengths to
ensure your soups, starters, and salads are flavorsome
without tipping the scales. Dig your fork into the
glorious colors of Salade Nicoise, plunge your spoon
into the delicious depths of Indian Spiced Potato and
Onion Soup, or sink your teeth into the fabulous
textures of Mixed Mushrooms on Herbed Muffins.
Tackle the kitchen with a new determination because
you will enjoy each morsel – and if you think things
couldn't get any better than this, remember, we're
only getting started…

Salade Nicoise

Serves 4
Preparation 2 mins
Cooking 30 mins
Calories 400
Fat 3g

4 small waxy potatoes
2 cups fine green beans
3 medium eggs
4 tomatoes
12 white onions, thinly sliced
6 oz can tuna in oil, drained
8 black olives, halved
6 anchovy fillets (optional), halved
2 small lettuce, leaves separated
watercress sprigs to garnish

Dressing
4 tbsp sunflower oil or olive oil
1 tbsp white wine vinegar
salt and black pepper

1 Boil the potatoes in a saucepan of salted water for 15-20 minutes, until tender. Drain and set aside until cool enough to handle, then dice. Meanwhile, cook the beans in another saucepan of boiling salted water for 5 minutes or until tender. Drain and halve.
2 Put the eggs into a saucepan of cold water. Bring to the boil, then cook for 10 minutes. Peel the eggs under cold running water and cut into quarters lengthways. Place the tomatoes in a bowl and cover with boiling water. Leave for 30 seconds, then peel and cut into wedges.
3 Place the potatoes, green beans, eggs, tomatoes, onion, tuna, olives, and anchovies, if using, in a large bowl. Mix together the dressing ingredients, pour over the salad and toss lightly. Line a platter with the lettuce leaves and spoon the salad on top. Garnish with watercress.

Indian Spiced Potato and Onion Soup

1 tbsp vegetable oil
1 onion, finely chopped
$^1/_2$ in piece fresh root ginger,
finely chopped
2 large potatoes, cut into
$^1/_2$ in cubes
2 tsp ground cumin
2 tsp ground cilantro
$^1/_2$ tsp turmeric
1 tsp ground cinnamon
4 cups chicken stock
salt and black pepper
1 tbsp natural yogurt to garnish

1 Heat the oil in a large saucepan. Fry the onion and ginger for 5 minutes or until softened. Add potatoes, fry for another minute, stirring often.

2 Mix the cumin, cilantro, turmeric, and cinnamon with 2 tablespoons of cold water to make a paste. Add to onion and potato, stirring well, fry 1 minute to release flavors.

3 Add stock and season to taste. Bring to boil, then reduce the heat, cover and simmer for 30 minutes or until the potato is tender. Blend until smooth in a food processor or press through a metal sieve. Return to the pan and gently heat through. Garnish with the yogurt and more black pepper.

Note: This delicately spiced soup makes a great start to an Indian meal. Also makes a satisfying snack on its own, when served with warm naan bread and a salad.

Serves 4
Preparation 10 mins
Cooking 40 mins
Calories 136
Fat <1g

Thai Hot and Sour Shrimp Soup

Serves 4
Preparation 25 mins
Cooking 30 mins
Calories 152
Fat <1g

2 stalks lemon grass
³/₄ lb whole raw shell-on shrimp, defrosted if frozen
1 tbsp vegetable oil
4 cups chicken stock
1 clove garlic, crushed
1 inch piece fresh root ginger, chopped
grated rind of 1 lime and juice of 2 limes
1 green chili, deseeded and finely chopped
salt and black pepper
1 tbsp Thai fish sauce
1 red chili, deseeded and sliced, and 2 tbsp chopped fresh cilantro to garnish

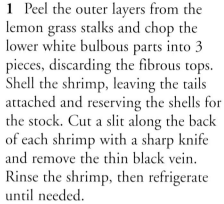

1 Peel the outer layers from the lemon grass stalks and chop the lower white bulbous parts into 3 pieces, discarding the fibrous tops. Shell the shrimp, leaving the tails attached and reserving the shells for the stock. Cut a slit along the back of each shrimp with a sharp knife and remove the thin black vein. Rinse the shrimp, then refrigerate until needed.

2 Heat the oil in a large saucepan. Fry shrimp shells for 2-3 minutes, until pink. Add the stock, garlic, ginger, lemon grass, lime rind, green chili, and salt to taste. Bring to the boil, then reduce the heat, cover and simmer for 20 minutes.

3 Strain the stock and return to the pan. Stir in the fish sauce and lime juice and bring to the boil. Add the shrimp, reduce the heat and simmer for 3 minutes, or until the shrimp turn pink and are cooked through. Season with pepper and serve garnished with red chili and cilantro.

Thai-Style Shellfish and Pomelo Salad

1 pomelo or 2 pink grapefruit
$^1\!/_2$ lb cooked peeled shrimp
6 oz can crabmeat in brine,
drained
1 small lettuce, chopped
1 spring onion, finely chopped

Dressing
1 tbsp groundnut oil
1 clove garlic, finely chopped
1 shallot, finely chopped
1 red chili, deseeded
and finely chopped
2 tbsp Thai fish sauce
2 tbsp dark brown sugar
juice of 1 lime

1 First make the dressing. Heat the oil in a small frying pan. Fry the garlic, shallot, and chili for 3 minutes or until the garlic has turned pale golden and the shallot has softened. Mix together the fish sauce, sugar and lime juice, stir in the shallot mixture, then set aside for 5 minutes to cool.
2 Using a sharp knife, slice off the top and bottom of the pomelo or grapefruit, then remove the skin and pith, following the curve of the fruit. Cut between the membranes to release the segments.
3 Mix the pomelo or grapefruit segments with the shrimp (prawns), crabmeat, and lettuce. Pour over the dressing and toss, then sprinkle over the spring onion.

Note: Pomelos look like grapefruit but have a sweeter flesh. If you can't get them, use pink grapefruit which goes just as well with the crab and shrimp (prawns) in this fresh, light salad.

Serves 4
Preparation 25 mins plus
5 mins cooling
Cooking nil
Calories 221
Fat <1g

Pikelets with Smoked Salmon and Horseradish

Note: Pikelets are small batter pancakes similar to Russian blinis. Their texture makes them perfect partners for smoked salmon and creamy horseradish.

Serves 4
Preparation 10 mins
Cooking 5 mins
Calories 139
Fat <1g

¹/₂ cup crème fraîche
1 tbsp creamed horseradish
1 tbsp chopped fresh dill, extra to garnish
squeeze of fresh lemon juice
1 tsp clear honey
salt and black pepper
8 pikelets
¹/₂ lb smoked salmon slices

1 Preheat the grill to high. In a bowl, combine the crème fraîche, horseradish, dill, lemon juice, and honey, then season with salt and pepper.
2 Toast the pikelets under the grill for 1-2 minutes, until golden, then turn them over and cook for a further 1-2 minutes. Top each pikelet with a spoonful of the crème fraîche mixture, some smoked salmon and a sprinkling of black pepper. Serve garnished with dill.

Photograph on page 13

Parsnip and Apple Soup with Garlic Croutons

Note: Parsnips and apples give this smooth thick soup a natural sweetness. Just serve it with chunks of crusty bread if you don't want to make the croutons.

Serves 4
Preparation 20 mins
Cooking 30 mins
Calories 284
Fat 2.9g

2 tbsp vegetable oil
1 onion, chopped
2 parsnips, chopped
1 cooking apple, chopped
2¹/₂ cups vegetable stock
2 tbsp chopped fresh parsley, plus extra to garnish
¹/₂ tsp dried marjoram
2 cups milk
salt and black pepper

Croutons
2 thick slices day-old white bread, no crusts
1 clove garlic, halved
2 tbsp vegetable oil

1 Heat the oil in a large heavy-based saucepan. Add onion and parsnips and cook for 5 minutes or until softened. Add the apple, stock, parsley and marjoram, bring to the boil. Cover, simmer for 20 minutes or until vegetables are tender.
2 Meanwhile, make the croutons. Rub both sides of each slice of bread with a half-clove of garlic. Cut the bread into ¹/₂ inch cubes. Heat the oil in a heavy-based frying pan. Add the bread and fry for 2-3 minutes, until golden, stirring constantly. Drain on kitchen towels.
3 Remove the soup from the heat. Stir in the milk and season to taste. Blend until smooth in a food processor or with a hand blender. Reheat and serve with croutons. Garnish with the parsley.

Chef's Fall Salad

Note: Chef's Salad can have almost anything in it. This one makes good use of colorful fresh vegetables and apples, and comes with a zingy lime and cilantro dressing.

Serves 4
Preparation 30 mins plus 15 mins cooling
Cooking 2 mins
Calories 330
Fat 2.5g

salt and black pepper
1/2 lb broccoli, cut into small florets
1 romaine lettuce, leaves torn
1 red onion, halved and sliced
12 cucumbers, peeled and diced
2 sticks celery, sliced
2 carrots, cut into matchsticks
2 apples, diced
1/2 lb wafer-thin cooked turkey or ham slices
2 tbsp each raisins and roasted salted peanuts, chopped (optional)

Dressing
1 tsp Dijon mustard
juice of 1/2 lime
5/8 cup low-fat natural yogurt
2 tbsp olive oil
1 tbsp chopped fresh cilantro seasoning

1 Bring a large saucepan of salted water to a boil. Add the broccoli, return to a boil, then cook for 1-2 minutes, until slightly softened. Drain and leave to cool for 15 minutes. Meanwhile, make dressing. Mix together the mustard, lime juice, yogurt, oil, and cilantro seasoning.

2 Place the lettuce, red onion, cucumber, broccoli, celery, carrots, and apples in a large bowl. Pour over dressing and toss to coat. Arrange turkey and ham slices in centre of a shallow serving dish or platter and spoon the salad around the edge. Scatter over the raisins and peanuts.

Serves 4 **Preparation** 20 mins **Cooking** 10 mins **Calories** 286 **Fat** 2.3g

Vegetable Toasts with Tomato Dressing

**2 zucchini, thinly sliced
lengthways
2 carrots, thinly sliced lengthways
2 red bell peppers, deseeded and
thinly sliced
sea salt and freshly ground black
pepper
4 thick slices white loaf
1 tbsp sunflower oil**

Dressing
**2 tomatoes
4 tbsp virgin olive oil
2 spring onions, sliced
1 tbsp white wine vinegar**

1 Place the zucchini, carrots, and red bell peppers in a bowl and season well. (You can use a vegetable peeler to make long ribbons with zucchini and carrots.)

2 Toast the bread for 3 minutes each side or until golden brown. Meanwhile, for the dressing, place the tomatoes, in a bowl of boiling water for 30 seconds, then peel, deseed and finely chop.

3 Heat the sunflower oil in a large frying pan over a high heat, cook the vegetables for 4 minutes, stirring all the time, until they have softened and are just tender. Remove and set aside.

4 In the same pan, heat the olive oil, and add the spring onions and white wine vinegar. Cook, stirring occasionally, for 1–2 minutes, until hot, then stir in the tomatoes. Pile the vegetables on top of the toasts, drizzle with the hot dressing and serve.

Note: The dressing, drizzled over the pan-fried vegetables, soaks into the crispy toast, making a stunning dinner party starter. Smaller versions make fabulous canapés. Beta carotene is the antioxidant and pigment found in many great-tasting brightly colored vegetables. Tomatoes get their color from a different but particularly potent antioxidant pigment called lycopene.

Roasted Vegetable Salad

OVEN TEMPERATURE
400°F, 200°C, GAS 6

Note: This salad combines a healthy mix of the antioxidant vitamins A, C, and E, plus bags of minerals from the great-tasting vegetables. Remember, the more brightly-colored the vegetables are, the more nutrients they are likely to contain. Roasting vegetables brings out their flavor and really intensifies their natural sweetness. Serve with plenty of fresh, crusty bread to soak up the yummy dressing.

Serves 4
Preparation 15 mins
Cooking 35 mins
Calories 402
Fat 2.67g

3 red onions, quartered
3 potatoes, scrubbed and cut into wedges
2 zucchini, thickly sliced
2 yellow bell peppers deseeded and thickly sliced
4 tomatoes, halved
2 tbsp olive oil
sea salt and freshly ground black pepper
Parmesan shavings (optional)

Dressing
3 tbsp extra virgin olive oil
2 tbsp clear honey
1 tbsp balsamic vinegar
finely grated rind and juice of ¹/₂ lemon

1 Preheat the oven. Place all vegetables in a shallow roasting tin, drizzle over olive oil and season. Shake the tray gently to ensure vegetables are well coated with oil and seasoning. Bake for about 35 minutes, until the vegetables are really tender and slightly charred at the edges.
2 Meanwhile, mix all the dressing ingredients together and pour this over the roasted vegetables, toss well, and divide onto four plates. Top with Parmesan shavings, if using.

Thai Fish Sticks with Cucumber Salad

4 spring onions, chopped
small handful of fresh cilantro
1 lb cod loin or other skinless
white fish fillet, cubed
3 tbsp red curry paste
1 tsp salt
2 tsp lime juice
1 large egg white
12 stalks lemon grass

Salad
¹/₂ cucumber, peeled and
very thinly sliced
4 tbsp white wine vinegar
4 tbsp white sugar
1 large red or green chili,
deseeded and chopped
1 small shallot, sliced
4 tbsp cold water

1 To make the salad, combine the cucumber, vinegar, sugar, chili, and shallot with 4 tablespoons of cold water. Cover and leave in a cool place until needed.
2 To make fish sticks, blend spring onions and cilantro in a food processor until finely chopped. Add the fish, curry paste, salt, and lime juice, and blend until the fish is finely chopped. Add the egg white and continue blending until the mixture is stiff.
3 Divide the fish mixture into 12 portions, then carefully press each around a lemon grass stick, forming a "sausage" shape. Preheat the grill to high. Place the fish sticks on a lightly oiled baking sheet, then grill for 6 minutes, turning once, until cooked and lightly browned on all sides. Serve with the cucumber salad.

Note: Cooking these spicy kebabs on lemon grass sticks gives them a lovely citrus flavor. The simple salad combines slivers of cool cucumber with a little red-hot chili.

Serves 4
Preparation 2 mins
Cooking 6 mins
Calories 200
Fat <1g

Mixed Mushrooms on Herbed Muffins

1 lb mixed mushrooms, including
wild, oyster and shiitake
2 tbsp olive oil
salt and black pepper
2 tbsp butter
1 clove garlic, crushed
3 tbsp chopped fresh parsley
3 tbsp finely snipped chives, plus
extra whole chives to garnish
2 tsp sherry vinegar or
balsamic vinegar
4 tbsp low-fat soft cheese
3 English white muffins

1 Halve any large mushrooms. Heat 2 teaspoons of the oil in a heavy-based frying pan, then add all mushrooms, season lightly, and fry over a medium to high heat for 5 minutes or until they start to release their juices.
2 Remove the mushrooms and drain on kitchen towels, then set aside. Add the rest of the oil and half the butter to the pan, and heat until the butter melts. Add the garlic and stir for 1 minute.
3 Return the mushrooms to the pan, then increase the heat to high and fry for 5 minutes or until they are tender and starting to crisp. Stir in remaining butter and 2 tablespoons each of parsley and chives, drizzle with the vinegar, and season.
4 Mix the soft cheese with the remaining parsley and snipped chives. Split and toast the muffins. Spread the soft cheese mixture over the muffin halves and place on serving plates. Top with the mushrooms and garnish with the whole chives.

Serves 6
Preparation 10 mins
Cooking 10 mins
Calories 145
Fat 3g

Cajun Chicken Brochettes

**3 large skinless boneless chicken
breasts, cut into 1 in pieces
salt and black pepper
olive oil for brushing
skewers**

Marinade
**3 tbsp Dijon mustard
3 tbsp clear honey
1 tbsp olive oil
2 tbsp tomato ketchup
$^1/_2$ tsp Tabasco
1 clove garlic, crushed
$^1/_2$ tsp dried thyme
3 basil leaves, finely chopped, plus
extra leaves to garnish**

Peach Salsa
**3 peaches, fresh or canned
$^2/_3$ cup natural yogurt
1 tsp lemon juice**

1 To make marinade, mix mustard,
honey, oil, ketchup, Tabasco, garlic,
thyme, and basil in a shallow non-
metallic dish that is large enough to
hold 6 skewers. If using wooden
skewers, soak them in water for 10
minutes.

2 Season the chicken pieces with a
little salt and pepper, then thread
onto the skewers. Add to the
marinade and turn until coated.
Cover and place in the fridge for
1 hour, stirring occasionally.

3 Meanwhile, make the peach salsa.
If using fresh peaches, put them into
a bowl, cover with boiling water, and
leave for 30 seconds. Peel off the
skins, remove the stones and chop.
If using canned peaches, chop the
flesh. Mix the peaches with the
yogurt and lemon juice, season with
black pepper, cover and refrigerate
until needed.

4 Preheat the grill to high and brush
the rack with oil. Place the
brochettes on the grill rack, brush
with half the marinade and grill for
6 minutes. Turn them over, brush
with the rest of the marinade and
grill for a further 2-3 minutes, until
the chicken is tender and cooked
through. Serve with the salsa,
garnished with basil.

*Note: Tender chunks
of chicken in a
piquant marinade
are set off by a peach
and yogurt salsa.
You'll love it so
much you may want
to double the
quantities and serve
it as a main course.*

Serves 4
Preparation 25 mins
plus 1 hr marinating
Cooking 10 mins
Calories 312
Fat 1.3g

Meat and Poultry

Boldly blend seasonings and marinades that will glaze pork, roast chicken, and stir-fry beef like never before. Main meals with meat and poultry can be appetizing without layering them with fat-ridden ingredients, so you feel convinced that a good feed *can* come guilt-free. As you explore each recipe, you will realize that low-fat cuisine can be creative without compromising on taste or quality. Let us guide you on a wonderful journey towards greater health as you learn to take a fresh approach to eating, and cultivate a new appreciation for homemade meat and poultry dishes. It's all at your fingertips…

Lamb Osso Bucco

OVEN TEMPERATURE
325°F, 160°C, GAS 3

Note: The lamb is cooked very slowly in this Italian recipe, leaving it meltingly tender, and there should be enough to satisfy the biggest of appetites. Serve with pasta ribbons.

**2 tbsp plain flour
salt and black pepper
4 lamb leg shanks,
trimmed of excess fat
2 tbsp olive oil
1 onion, finely chopped
1 carrot, finely chopped
1 stick celery, chopped
2 cups canned chopped tomatoes
with garlic and herbs
1 tbsp sun-dried tomato purée
⁵/₈ cup dry white wine
2 cups lamb stock**

Garnish
**1 tbsp chopped fresh parsley
1 tbsp chopped fresh mint
finely grated rind of 1 lemon
1 clove garlic, finely chopped**

1 Preheat the oven. Mix together the flour, salt, and pepper on a plate. Dip lamb pieces into mixture to coat well. Heat 1 tablespoon of oil in large heavy-based frying pan until hot, but not smoking. Add the coated lamb and cook over a medium to high heat for 5-8 minutes, turning frequently, until browned on all sides. Transfer to a deep ovenproof dish.
2 Heat the remaining oil in the pan, add onion, carrot, and celery and cook over a low heat for 4-5 minutes, until softened. Add tomatoes, tomato purée, wine and stock, bring to boil, stirring occasionally. Pour over lamb, cover with foil and bake for 1³/₄-2 hours, until the meat is tender, turning it over halfway through. Season to taste.
3 To make garnish, mix together parsley, mint, lemon rind, and garlic. Sprinkle garnish over lamb and serve.

Serves 4
Preparation 15 mins
Cooking 2 hrs 15 mins
Calories 479
Fat 5g

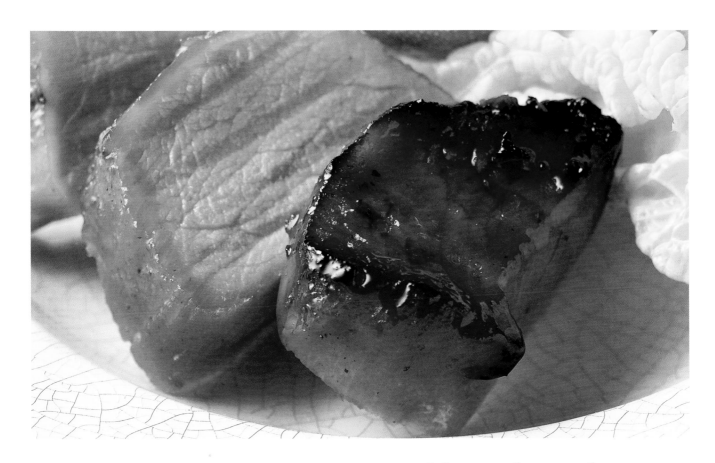

Cantonese Honey-Glazed Pork

**1 lb rindless boneless pork loin,
cut into 2 inch wide pieces**

Marinade
**2 cloves garlic
1 tsp salt
2 tbsp light soy sauce
3 tbsp sugar
1 tbsp medium dry sherry
^{1}/$_2$ tsp Chinese five-spice
powder (optional)
1 tsp hoisin sauce
1 tbsp clear honey**

1 To make marinade, crush garlic
with salt, then mix with the rest of
the marinade ingredients in a non-
metallic bowl. Score each piece of
pork a few times with a sharp knife,
add to marinade, and turn to coat.
Cover and refrigerate for 4 hours,
or overnight, turning occasionally.

2 Preheat the oven. Half-fill a deep
roasting pan with boiling water and
place the pork on a rack over the
top, ensuring that the meat does
not touch the water. Brush the pork
with half the marinade and roast for
30 minutes.
3 Reduce the heat to
350°F/180°C/Gas Mark 4. Turn
the pork over and brush with the
remaining marinade. Roast for
another 30 minutes until pork is
cooked through and tender. Slice
into ^{1}/$_2$ inch thick pieces to serve.

OVEN TEMPERATURE
400°F, 200°C, GAS 6

*Note: This Chinese
glazed pork has a
rich barbecue flavor
that really brings
out the sweetness of
the meat.
Serve with a wedge
of lime and crisp
Chinese leaves.*

Serves 4
Preparation 10 mins
plus 4 hrs marinating
Cooking 1 hr
Calories 240
Fat 2.5g

Roasted Tandoori Chicken Breasts

**4 skinless boneless
chicken breasts**

Marinade
**1 tsp salt
2 cloves garlic, chopped
1 inch piece fresh
root ginger, chopped
1 tbsp chopped fresh cilantro,
plus extra leaves to garnish
1 tbsp chopped fresh mint
$^1\!/_2$ tsp turmeric
$^1\!/_2$ tsp hot chili powder
2 cardamom pods, split, husks
discarded and seeds reserved
4 tbsp natural yogurt
juice of $^1\!/_2$ lemon**

1 For marinade, grind salt, garlic, ginger, cilantro, mint, turmeric, chili powder and cardamom seeds to a paste, using a pestle and mortar or coffee grinder. Transfer to a large, non-metallic bowl, stir in the yogurt and lemon juice, and mix together well.
2 Score each chicken breast 4 times with a sharp knife, then add to the bowl and turn to coat thoroughly. Cover and chill for 6 hours, or overnight.
3 Preheat the oven. Place the chicken breasts on a rack in a roasting pan and cook for 20-25 minutes, until they are tender and the juices run clear when pierced with a skewer.

Photograph on page 24

OVEN TEMPERATURE
425°F, 220°C, GAS 7

Note: This is a simplified version of the traditional Indian recipe, but fresh herbs and lots of spice ensure it's just as tasty as the real thing. Serve with naan bread and salad.

Serves 4
Preparation 15 mins
plus 6 hrs marinating
Cooking 25 mins
Calories 135
Fat 0.50g

Japanese Pan-Fried Glazed Chicken

**1 tbsp groundnut oil
4 skinless boneless chicken
breasts, sliced diagonally
spring onions, shredded
to garnish**

Glaze
**$^1\!/_2$ cup dark soy sauce
$^1\!/_2$ cup rice wine or
medium-dry sherry
3 tbsp granulated sugar**

1 To make the glaze, place the soy sauce, rice wine or sherry, and the sugar into a small saucepan. Cook gently for 3 minutes or until the sugar has dissolved, stirring.
2 Heat the oil in a large, heavy-based frying pan. Fry the chicken for 3-5 minutes, until lightly colored. Pour over the glaze.
3 Fry for 5 minutes or until the glaze has nearly evaporated and chicken pieces are coated and cooked through, turning occasionally. Serve garnished with spring onions.

Note: This sweet glazed dish comes from Japan where it's known as teriyaki. The recipe works equally well with beef or pork, and is traditionally served with rice.

Serves 4
Preparation 5 mins
Cooking 15 mins
Calories 247
Fat 0.77g

Chicken with Lemon Cilantro Couscous

Serves 4
Preparation 15 mins
plus 10 mins soaking
Cooking 10 mins
Calories 517
Fat 5g

wooden skewers
**4 large skinless boneless chicken
breasts, cut into 1 inch cubes**
1 tbsp olive oil
1 clove garlic, crushed
**1 tsp each of ground cilantro,
ginger and cinnamon**
pinch of cayenne pepper
$^1/_2$ tsp salt
juice of 1$^1/_2$ lemons
2 cups couscous
2 tbsp butter
**2 tbsp chopped fresh cilantro, plus
extra leaves to garnish**
**6 tbsp pitted black
olives, chopped**
black pepper
lemon wedges to serve

1 Soak 4 wooden skewers in water for at least 10 minutes. Toss the chicken with the oil, garlic, ground spices, cayenne, salt, and 1 tablespoon of lemon juice until the pieces are evenly coated.

2 Preheat the grill to high. Thread the chicken onto the skewers and grill for 8-10 minutes, turning occasionally, until slightly charred, cooked through and tender. Keep warm.

3 Meanwhile, prepare the couscous according to packet instructions, then fluff it up with a fork. Stir the butter, remaining lemon juice, cilantro, and olives into couscous and season. Transfer to serving plates, top with chicken, and drizzle over any pan juices. Serve with the lemon wedges and garnish with cilantro.

Spiced Lamb and Apricot Pilau

1 tbsp vegetable oil
1 onion, chopped
2 cloves garlic, chopped
1 lb neck of lamb or stewing lamb
off the bone, cut into 1 inch cubes
1 tsp turmeric
1 tsp ground cumin
$^1/_2$ tsp ground cinnamon
1 tbsp grated fresh root ginger
$1^1/_4$ cups long-grain white rice
2 cups canned chopped tomatoes
$1^1/_4$ cups vegetable or lamb stock
$^3/_4$ cup ready-to-eat dried apricots,
chopped
$^1/_3$ cup seedless raisins
salt and black pepper
3 tbsp toasted flaked almonds
(optional)

1 Heat the oil in a large heavy-based saucepan and cook the onion, garlic and lamb for 5 minutes, or until the onion and garlic have softened and the meat has browned. Stir in the turmeric, cumin, cinnamon, and ginger, then cook for 1 minute, stirring, to release their flavors.
2 Add rice and cook, stirring for 1 minute to coat well. Add tomatoes and half the stock, then stir in apricots and raisins. Cover and cook gently for 10 minutes, checking mixture from time to time and adding a little more stock if it starts to dry out.

Add half of the remaining stock and cook for a further 10 minutes. Then add the rest of the stock and cook for 30-35 minutes, stirring, until the rice is tender and all the liquid is absorbed. Add a little extra water if the mixture becomes too dry.
3 Season to taste and remove from the heat. Cover and leave to stand for 5 minutes. Serve sprinkled with toasted almonds, if desired.

Note: In this dish, apricots, long-grain rice and tender chunks of lamb are simmered in a spicy stock. And it's all cooked in one pot so there's hardly any washing up.

Serves 4
Preparation 20 mins
plus 5 mins standing
Cooking 1 hr
Calories 625
Fat 3g

Stir-Fried Noodles with Pork and Ginger

Note: You can really smell the fresh ginger in this quick and easy Chinese dish. The sherry adds a little sweetness to the tangy sauce, which coats the pork and noodles.

Serves 4
Preparation 15 mins
Cooking 15 mins
Calories 874
Fat 9g

16 oz Chinese egg noodles
¹/₂ lb fresh ground pork
1 tbsp soy sauce
1 tbsp dry sherry
1 tsp cornflour
2 tbsp vegetable oil
2 spring onions, chopped,
plus extra to garnish
1 tsp finely grated
fresh root ginger
1 carrot, finely chopped
3 tbsp black bean sauce
¹/₂ cup chicken stock

1 Cook the noodles according to packet instructions, then drain well. In a bowl, mix together the pork, soy sauce, sherry and cornflour. Stir well to combine.

2 Heat the oil in a wok or large heavy-based frying pan, then add the spring onions and ginger and stir-fry for 30 seconds. Add the pork mixture and the carrot and stir-fry for 5-10 minutes, until the pork has browned. Stir in the bean sauce.

3 Pour in the stock and bring to a boil. Add the noodles and cook, uncovered, for 3-5 minutes, until most of the liquid is absorbed and the noodles are piping hot. Garnish with spring onions.

Yorkshire Pudding in Ground Beef

¹/₂ cup plain flour
salt and black pepper
2 medium eggs
1¹/₄ cups milk
2 tbsp vegetable oil
1 onion, chopped
1 carrot, chopped
1 cup mushrooms, chopped
³/₄ lb ground beef
1 cup canned chopped tomatoes
1 cup baked beans
fresh parsley to garnish

1 Sift flour and pinch of salt into a bowl, then make a well in the center. Break eggs into the well. Beat eggs gradually drawing in the flour and adding milk a little at a time until it forms a smooth batter. Cover and leave for 30 minutes.

2 Preheat the oven. Heat 1 tablespoon of oil in a large, heavy-based frying pan and cook onion and carrot for 5 minutes or until softened. Add mushrooms and cook for 2-3 minutes, then stir in beef and cook for 5 minutes or until browned. Add tomatoes and cook for 15 minutes. Stir in baked beans, heat for 5 minutes, season and keep warm.

3 Meanwhile, divide the remaining oil between 4 Yorkshire pudding tins. Place in the oven for 5 minutes or until the oil is hot. Pour in the batter and cook for 20-25 minutes, until risen and crisp. Place on serving plates, spoon in the ground beef, and garnish with parsley.

OVEN TEMPERATURE
425°F, 220°C, GAS 7

Note: These Yorkshire pudding cases are delicious with a variety of fillings—try them with chicken curry, meatballs in tomato sauce, or a thick vegetable ratatouille.

Serves 4
Preparation 15 mins plus 30 mins standing
Cooking 35 mins
Calories 423
Fat 9g

Mexican-Style Beef Olives

OVEN TEMPERATURE
300°F, 150°C, GAS 2

Note: A little beef goes a long way in this twist on chili con carne. Serve it with bread or mashed potatoes.

Serves 4
Preparation 20 mins
Cooking 1hr 45 mins
Calories 433
Fat 9g

4 thin-cut beef steaks
4 rashers rindless bacon, finely chopped
1 tbsp chopped fresh parsley
$^1/_2$ tsp dried marjoram
1 cup fresh breadcrumbs
$^1/_2$ cup flour
salt and black pepper
packet of cocktail sticks
1 tbsp vegetable oil
1-2 tsp hot chili powder
1 onion, chopped
2 cloves garlic, finely chopped
1 red bell pepper, deseeded and chopped
1 cup beef stock
2 cups canned red kidney beans, drained and rinsed

1 Preheat the oven. Place the beef between sheets of cling film and flatten slightly with a rolling pin. Put bacon into a large frying pan and fry gently for 2-3 minutes, until cooked. Remove from heat and stir in parsley, marjoram and breadcrumbs.

2 Mix together flour, salt, and pepper in a shallow dish. Divide the bacon mixture between slices of beef, then roll up each slice from the short end, turn in seasoned flour, and secure with a wetted cocktail stick.

3 Heat the oil in a flameproof casserole dish, add the beef, and cook for 2 minutes, turning until browned all over. Remove from the dish and set aside. Add the chili powder, onion, garlic, and red bell pepper to the dish, and cook for 3 minutes to soften. Return the meat to the dish, pour in the stock, and then bring to a boil. Cover the dish, then bake for 45 minutes. Add the kidney beans and cook for another 45 minutes. Remove the cocktail sticks and serve.

Turkey and Mushroom Creole

1 tbsp olive oil
1 onion, chopped
2 cloves garlic, chopped
1 red bell pepper, deseeded and chopped
2 sticks celery, chopped
2 cups canned chopped tomatoes
1 tsp chili powder
large pinch of cayenne pepper
1 tsp paprika
$1/4$ tsp dried thyme
1 lb quick-cook turkey steaks, cut into strips
1 cup button mushrooms, sliced

1 Heat the oil in a large heavy-based saucepan, then add the onion, garlic, red bell pepper, and celery, and cook gently for 10 minutes or until softened.
2 Stir in the tomatoes, chili, cayenne, paprika, and thyme and heat through for 1-2 minutes to release the flavors. Stir in the turkey strips and mushrooms, then cover the pan and cook gently for 30 minutes, stirring occasionally, until the turkey is cooked through and tender.

Note: This West Indian-inspired dish tastes great and it's really healthy, too. Serve it with some rice to soak up the spicy tomato and mushroom sauce.

Serves 4
Preparation 20 mins
Cooking 45 mins
Calories 246
Fat 1.15g

Beef with Black Bean Sauce

Note: Black bean sauce is fabulous with beef – it makes all the difference to this stir fry.
To carry on the Chinese theme, you can serve this dish with egg noodles or plain rice.

Serves 4
Preparation 15 mins
Cooking 15 mins
Calories 275
Fat 2.5g

1 lb sirloin or rump steak, cut into thin strips
1 clove garlic, crushed
1 small red chili, deseeded and finely chopped
1 tbsp dark soy sauce
black pepper
2 tsp cornflour
1 tbsp water
1 tbsp white wine vinegar
2 tbsp vegetable oil
1 yellow and 1 red bell pepper, deseeded and cut into strips
1 large zucchini, cut into matchsticks
2 cups snowpeas, sliced
3 tbsp black bean stir-fry sauce
4 spring onions, sliced

1 Combine the steak strips, garlic, chili (if using), soy sauce and seasoning in a bowl. In another bowl, mix the cornflour with 1 tablespoon of water until smooth, then stir in the vinegar.

2 Heat the oil in a wok or large frying pan until very hot. Add the meat and its marinade and stir-fry for 4 minutes, tossing continuously, until it is seared on all sides.

3 Add the bell peppers and stir-fry for 2 minutes. Stir in the zucchini and snowpeas and cook for 3 minutes. Reduce the heat and add the cornflour mixture and black bean sauce. Stir to mix thoroughly, then cook for 2 minutes or until the meat and vegetables are cooked through. Scatter with the spring onions just before serving.

Duck Breasts with Chili

OVEN TEMPERATURE
425°F, 220°C, GAS 7

Note: Quickly pan-frying the duck, then roasting it, is a technique that a lot of chefs use to make the meat really succulent. Serve on a bed of bitter salad leaves or rocket.

Serves 4
Preparation 10 mins
plus 5 mins resting
Cooking 25 mins
Calories 196
Fat 1.9g

**4 boneless duck breasts,
about 5 oz each
juice of 2 large oranges,
plus few strips of rind to garnish
1 green chili, deseeded
and finely chopped
$1/_2$ cup dry vermouth
or sherry
1 tbsp redcurrant jelly
salt and black pepper**

1 Preheat oven. Score skin of each duck breast in a diamond pattern. Heat a heavy based frying pan until hot, place breasts, skinside down, in the pan. Cook over a medium to high heat for 5 minutes or until skin is browned and crispy.

2 Pour off the hot fat, turn over the duck, and cook for 5 minutes. Place the duck, skin-side up, on the rack of a roasting tin and cook in the oven for 10 minutes. Rest in a warm place for 5 minutes.
3 Meanwhile, make the dressing. Place the orange juice, chili, vermouth or sherry, redcurrant jelly, and seasoning in the pan. Boil vigorously, stirring constantly, for 5 minutes or until reduced and glossy.
4 Slice the duck very thinly. Serve with the sauce poured over and garnished with orange rind.

Mushrooms Stuffed with Pork and Sage

**8 very large open mushrooms
or 16 open cup mushrooms
1 tbsp vegetable oil
1 onion, finely chopped
2 cloves garlic, finely chopped
³/₄ lb fresh ground pork
2 cups fresh breadcrumbs
1 tbsp chopped fresh sage or
parsley, plus extra leaves
to garnish
1 medium egg, beaten
salt and black pepper**

Serves 4
Preparation 20 mins
Cooking 30 mins
Calories 216
Fat 4g

1 Preheat the oven. Remove any stalks from the mushrooms and finely chop. Heat the oil in a large heavy-based frying pan and fry the chopped mushroom stalks, onion, and garlic for 3-5 minutes, until softened. Add the pork and cook for 5 minutes, stirring, until the pork browns.
2 Transfer the mixture to a bowl. Stir in breadcrumbs, sage or parsley, and enough beaten egg to lightly bind the mixture. Season well.
3 Divide the stuffing between the mushrooms, using a spoon. Place on a baking sheet, bake for 20 minutes or until mushrooms have softened and the topping is golden. Scatter with the sage or parsley leaves.

OVEN TEMPERATURE
375°F, 190°C, GAS 5

Note: Large mushrooms are crammed with a delicious mixture of herby pork and golden breadcrumbs. Serve with a salad and some lightly buttered new potatoes.

Fish and Shellfish

If fish is the proverbial food for the brain, then you will be a genius when you realize how dishes from the deep can be tasty and still maintain a low-fat theme. Spice up salmon, cod, mussels, shrimp, and sardines to create scrumptious feasts that are perfect for family dining or adaptable to multi-guest entertaining. Stir fry shrimp with mango, grill salmon with horseradish, or bake cod with ginger for meals that are sure to please even the fussiest palate. So don your apron and fire up your oven because the pursuit of happiness never looked so good!

Oriental-Style Salmon Fillet

Note: Ginger, lime, and a little honey make a fabulous marinade for salmon. Its sweet and sour flavors go down well with children as well as adults. Serve with sugar snap peas.

Serves 4
Preparation 5 mins plus 10 mins marinating
Cooking 8 mins
Calories 426
Fat 4g

4 skinless salmon fillets
2 tbsp vegetable oil
2 tbsp light soy sauce
2 tbsp clear honey
1oz stem ginger, drained and finely chopped
2 spring onions, cut into long strips
finely grated rind and juice of $^1/_2$ lime
black pepper
lime wedges to serve

1 Place salmon fillets in a shallow non-metallic dish. Mix together oil, soy sauce, honey, ginger, spring onions, lime rind, and juice and seasoning. Pour over fillets and turn to coat. Cover and marinate in the fridge for 10 minutes, or 1 hour if you have time.
2 Preheat the grill to high. Lightly oil a baking tray. Lift the fillets and spring onions out of the marinade and place on the baking tray.
3 Brush the fillets with a little of the marinade, then cook for 3 minutes. Turn over, brush with more marinade and grill for 3-5 minutes, until cooked through. Serve with the lime.

Baked Cod with Ginger and Spring Onions

oil for greasing
1 lb piece cod fillet
1 tbsp light soy sauce
1 tbsp rice wine or
medium-dry sherry
1 tsp sesame oil
salt
3 spring onions, shredded and cut
into 1 inch pieces, white and
green parts separated
1 inch pieces fresh root ginger,
finely chopped

1   Preheat the oven. Line a shallow baking dish with a piece of lightly greased foil.

2   Place the cod in the dish, skin-side down. Pour over the soy sauce, rice wine or sherry, oil and salt to taste, then sprinkle over the white parts of the spring onion and the ginger.

3   Loosely wrap the foil over the fish, folding the edges together to seal. Bake for 20-25 minutes, until cooked through and tender. Unwrap the parcel, transfer fish to a serving plate and sprinkle over green parts of spring onions to garnish.

OVEN TEMPERATURE
375°F, 190°C, GAS 5

Note: One of the best ways to cook fish is to bake it in a foil parcel so that it cooks in its own juices. Here, sesame oil, ginger, and spring onions add a Chinese twist.

Serves 4
Preparation 10 mins
Cooking 25 mins
Calories 114
Fat trace

Chili-Spiked Mussels with Spaghetti

Note: A little bit of chili adds a spicy bite to the mussels, while garlic, parsley, and shallots mingle with the spaghetti. It's perfect served with fresh crusty bread.

Serves 4
Preparation 20 mins
Cooking 20 mins
Calories 621
Fat 2.6g

³/₄ **lb dried spaghetti**
2 lb fresh mussels
2 tbsp olive oil, plus 1 tbsp extra for drizzling
2 shallots, finely chopped
4 cloves garlic, chopped
¹/₂ **cup dry white wine**
grated rind of ¹/₂ **lemon**
¹/₂ **tsp dried chili flakes**
2 tbsp chopped fresh parsley
salt and black pepper

1 Cook pasta according to packet instructions, until tender but still firm to the bite, then drain well. Meanwhile, scrub the mussels under cold running water, pull away any beards and discard any mussels that are open or damaged.

2 Place mussels in a large heavy-based saucepan, with just the water clinging to the shells. Steam for 3-4 minutes over a high heat, shaking regularly, until shells have opened. Discard any mussels that remain closed.

3 Heat 2 tablespoons of oil in a large saucepan and gently fry the shallots and garlic for 5 minutes or until softened. Add the wine and boil rapidly for 5-6 minutes, until the liquid has reduced by half. Add the mussels, lemon rind, and chili, and heat for 2-3 minutes. Add the pasta to the mussels, then stir in the parsley and black pepper. Gently toss over heat and drizzle over the remaining oil.

South-East Asian Pan-Fried Shrimp

1 lb whole raw shell-on shrimp,
defrosted if frozen
3 small red chilies, deseeded and
chopped
2 cloves garlic, chopped
1 inch piece fresh root ginger,
chopped
1 shallot, chopped
2 tbsp groundnut oil
1 onion, chopped
2 tomatoes, quartered
1 tsp sugar
salt

1 Shell shrimp, leaving tails attached. Cut a slit along the back of each shrimp with a sharp knife, remove the thin black vein. Rinse well, then refrigerate until needed.
2 Blend the chilies, garlic, ginger, and shallot to a paste in a food processor or with a pestle and mortar. Heat the oil in a large, heavy-based frying pan or wok over a high heat, then fry the onion for 2 minutes to soften slightly. Add the paste and stir-fry for 1 minute to release the flavors.
3 Add the shrimp and tomatoes, mixing thoroughly, then sprinkle over the sugar and salt to taste. Fry for 3-5 minutes, until the shrimp turn pink and are cooked through, stirring often.

Note: It's well worth splashing out on large raw shrimp for this spicy dish. But ready-cooked shrimp are still tasty and take only a minute to warm through. Serve with rice.

Serves 4
Preparation 25 mins
Cooking 8 mins
Calories 224
Fat <1g

Salmon with Asparagus, Balsamic, and Orange

OVEN TEMPERATURE
400°F, 200°C, GAS 6

Note: The fresh tangy citrus flavors and balsamic vinegar cut through the richness of the salmon. Delicious, served simply with new potatoes. The rind of organic citrus fruit can be used in cooking without worrying about the wax, which non-organic fruit is sometimes sprayed with to make it shiny. Oranges are an excellent source of vitamin C.

Serves 4
Preparation 10 mins
Cooking 25 mins
Calories 395
Fat 4.6g

**2 tbsp extra virgin olive oil
finely grated rind of ¹/₂ orange,
plus the juice of 1 orange
sea salt and freshly ground
black pepper
¹/₂ lb bunch asparagus, trimmed
4 salmon steaks, weighing
about 6 oz each
1 tbsp balsamic vinegar
2 tbsp chopped fresh cilantro**

1 Preheat the oven. Place 1 tablespoon of the olive oil on a baking tray with grated orange rind and seasoning. Add asparagus and toss well in the oil mixture. Cook for 15–20 minutes or until tender.
2 Meanwhile, wash and wipe the salmon with kitchen paper and season. Heat the remaining oil in a large frying pan over a medium heat. Add the salmon to the pan and cook for 4–5 minutes each side, or until golden and cooked right through.
3 Add the balsamic vinegar and orange juice and simmer for about 2 minutes until the sauce is bubbling and warmed through, stir in the cilantro, and serve immediately with the asparagus.

Baked Cod with Herby Crust

3 tbsp vegetable oil, plus extra for greasing
2 cups fresh white breadcrumbs
finely grated rind and juice of
1 lime
4 tbsp chopped fresh parsley
2 tbsp chopped fresh chives
1 tsp Dijon mustard
1 tbsp finely grated fresh root ginger
black pepper
4 skinless cod fillets, about 6 oz each

1 Preheat the oven. Lightly grease a baking tray or ovenproof dish. Mix together the breadcrumbs, lime rind, parsley, chives, mustard, ginger, oil, and seasoning.
2 Place the cod fillets on the baking tray or in the dish and sprinkle with the lime juice, then season. Divide the topping between the fillets, pressing it firmly onto the fish.
3 Bake for 20 minutes or until the fish is cooked through and the topping is golden and crunchy.

OVEN TEMPERATURE
400°F, 200°C, GAS 6

Note: Parsley, chives, lime, and ginger all add their flavors to the crispy breadcrumb topping on these succulent cod fillets. Serve the dish with oven chips and tomatoes.

Serves 4
Preparation 15 mins
Cooking 20 mins
Calories 305
Fat 1.2g

Singapore Noodles with Shrimp and Ham

*Note: This colorful
oriental dish is an
irresistible mixture
of spicy noodles and
shrimp. You can add
some extra zest by
squeezing over a
little lime juice just
before serving.*

Serves 4
Preparation 35 mins
Cooking 10 mins
Calories 514
Fat 2g

$^1/_2$ **lb pack stir-fry rice noodles**
3 tbsp vegetable oil
1 red chili, deseeded, chopped
**4 tbsp Singapore
fried noodle paste**
2 tbsp white wine vinegar
1 tbsp sugar
**1 red bell pepper, deseeded and
thinly sliced**
**2 cups button mushrooms,
sliced**
8 oz cooked ham, cut into strips
$^1/_2$ **cup frozen peas**
**7 oz can water chestnuts, drained
and halved**
$^1/_2$ **lb raw peeled shrimp**
4 spring onions, finely sliced

1 Prepare the noodles according to
the packet instructions, then drain.
Heat the oil in a large wok or heavy-
based frying pan until very hot.
2 Add the chili, fried noodle paste,
vinegar and sugar to the pan and
cook for 1-2 minutes, stirring
constantly, to release the flavors.
Add the red bell pepper and
mushrooms, and stir-fry for 3
minutes or until the vegetables have
softened.
3 Add the ham, peas, water
chestnuts, and shrimp and stir-fry for
2-3 minutes, until shrimp turn pink.
Add the spring onions and noodles.
Cook for 1 minute, stirring, or until
the shrimp are cooked through and
everything is hot.

Crunchy Salmon Patties

14 oz pink salmon, tinned
3 spring onions, finely chopped
1¹/₂ cups fresh white breadcrumbs
3 tbsp chopped fresh parsley
2 tsp capers, drained
and finely chopped
1 tbsp creamed horseradish
1 medium egg, beaten
1 tbsp lemon juice
1 tbsp vegetable oil,
plus extra for brushing
black pepper
lemon wedges to serve

1 Drain the salmon, remove any skin and visible bones, then flake into a bowl. Mix with the spring onions, breadcrumbs, parsley, capers, horseradish, egg, lemon juice, vegetable oil, and seasoning, combining thoroughly. Divide mixture into 4 and shape into flat patties.

2 Preheat the grill to high. Grease a baking sheet. Place the patties on the baking sheet and brush the tops lightly with oil. Grill for 4-5 minutes, then turn over, brush with oil and grill for a further 5 minutes or until the patties are cooked through and lightly golden. Serve with the lemon wedges.

Note: There's just enough horseradish in these patties to give them a kick, without overpowering the subtle flavor of salmon. Serve with salad, chips, and some tartar sauce.

Serves 4
Preparation 15 mins
Cooking 10 mins
Calories 284
Fat 2.5g

Baked Cod Parcels

OVEN TEMPERATURE
400°F, 200°C, GAS 6

Note: Cooking fish in parcels is easy – and because all the flavors are sealed in, the result is fabulous. You can really taste the white wine, tomatoes, lemon, and parsley.

1 tbsp olive oil
1 small onion, thinly sliced
1 clove garlic, thinly sliced
1¹/₂ lb skinless cod fillet, cut into 4 equal pieces
3 tbsp chopped fresh parsley
1 lemon, thinly sliced
4 plum tomatoes, each cut lengthways into 8 pieces
salt and black pepper
4 tbsp dry white wine

1 Preheat the oven. Cut 4 double-thickness, 15 in square pieces of non-stick baking paper.
2 Heat oil in a frying pan, then fry onion and garlic for 2-3 minutes, until softened. Place a spoonful of the mixture in the center of each square of paper. Top with a piece of cod, sprinkle over the parsley, then arrange the lemon slices on top.
3 Divide the tomatoes between the paper squares. Season, then spoon over the wine. Lift opposite sides of the paper up and bring them over the filling, then fold over firmly at the top to make a sealed parcel. Place on a baking sheet and cook 20-25 minutes, until fish is tender and cooked.

Serves 4
Preparation 15 mins
Cooking 30 mins
Calories 66
Fat 0.5g

Sardines Stuffed with Spinach and Pine Nuts

8 fresh sardines
salt and black pepper
2 tbsp olive oil
1 shallot, finely chopped
1 tbsp pine nut kernels
2 cups frozen leaf spinach,
defrosted and excess moisture
squeezed out
1 tbsp golden raisins
2 tbsp fresh breadcrumbs
1 tbsp lime juice

1 Preheat oven. Remove scales from fish by scraping from tail end with the back of a small knife. Cut off the heads, then slice along belly and remove the guts. Open out each fish and place skin-side up on the worksurface. Press along the length of the backbone with your thumb, then turn the fish over and ease out the backbone, cutting it at the tail end but leaving the tail intact. Rinse and pat dry with kitchen towels, season, and turn in 1 tablespoon of the oil.

2 Heat the remaining oil in a frying pan and fry the shallot and pine nut kernels for 2-3 minutes, until golden. Remove from the heat, then stir in the spinach, golden raisins, 1 tablespoon of the breadcrumbs, and the lime juice. Season, then use the mixture to sandwich sardines together in pairs, skin-side out.

3 Lay the sardines on a baking sheet, sprinkle with remaining breadcrumbs, and bake for 10 minutes, or until golden and cooked through.

OVEN TEMPERATURE
425°F, 220°C, GAS 7

Serves 4
Preparation 25 mins
Cooking 15 mins
Calories 252
Fat 2.6g

Tiger Shrimp, Snowpeas, and Mango Stir-Fry

1 lb raw peeled tiger shrimp,
defrosted if frozen, rinsed and
dried
2 tbsp vegetable oil
1¹/₂ tbsp finely grated fresh root
ginger
3 cups snowpeas
bunch of spring onions, sliced
1 large ripe mango, peeled and
thinly sliced
2 tbsp light soy sauce

1   Cut a slit along the back of each
shrimp with a sharp knife and
remove any thin black vein.
2   Heat the oil in a wok, add the
ginger and shrimp and stir-fry for 2
minutes or until the shrimp are just
turning pink. Add the snowpeas
and spring onions and stir-fry for a
further minute to soften slightly.
Stir in the mango and soy sauce and
stir-fry for 1 minute to heat
through.

*Note: Succulent
shrimp, crunchy
snowpeas and juicy
mango are flavored
with soy sauce and
fresh ginger. Best of
all, you can get this
dish on the table in
20 minutes. Serve
with rice.*

Serves 4
Preparation 15 mins
Cooking 1 mins
Calories 237
Fat 0.85g

Seared Tuna with Roasted Plum Tomato

Oven temperature
425°F, 220°C, Gas 7

Note: Lightly pan-fried tuna is delicious with just a squeeze of lemon or lime juice.
But it's the roasted tomatoes, scented with rosemary, that make this dish so hard to beat.

Serves 4
Preparation 15 mins
plus 30 mins
marinating
Cooking 25 mins
Calories 383
Fat 4g

1 clove garlic, finely chopped
finely grated rind and
juice of 1 lime
5 tbsp olive oil, plus extra
for greasing
3 tbsp chopped rosemary
4 tuna steaks, about 5 oz each
and ³/₄ inch thick
6 plum tomatoes, halved
lengthways
1 red onion, halved and thinly
sliced lengthways
salt and black pepper

1 Mix together garlic, lime rind, half the lime juice, two tablespoons of oil, and 1 tablespoon of rosemary in a large dish. Add tuna and turn to coat evenly. Cover and place in the fridge for 30 minutes to marinate.

2 Preheat the oven. Place the tomatoes and onion in a shallow ovenproof dish with the remaining rosemary. Drizzle with the remaining oil and season. Roast in the oven for 15-20 minutes, until tender and lightly browned.
3 Lightly oil a ridged cast-iron grill pan or large frying pan and heat over a fairly high heat. Add the tuna and cook for 4-5 minutes, turning once, or until golden. Serve with the tomatoes and onion, sprinkled with the remaining lime juice.

Lemon-Scented Fish Pie

2 lb potatoes, cut into even-sized
pieces
salt and black pepper
4 tbsp butter
1 onion, chopped
2 sticks celery, sliced
2 tbsp plain flour
1 cup fish stock
finely grated rind and juice
of 1 large lemon
1 lb cod loin, cubed
$^1\!/_2$ lb cooked and shelled mussels
2 tbsp chopped fresh parsley
4 tbsp milk

Serves 4
Preparation 20 mins
Cooking 1 hr
Calories 532
Fat 7g

OVEN TEMPERATURE
425°F, 220°C, GAS 7

*Note: Creamy
mashed potatoes
make a wonderful
topping for this
lemon-flavored cod
and mussel pie. If
you want to, replace
the mussels with
peeled shrimp.*

1 Cook the potatoes in boiling
salted water for 15-20 minutes,
until tender, then drain.
2 Meanwhile, melt $^1\!/_3$ of the butter
in a large saucepan, then add the
onion and celery and cook for 2-3
minutes, until softened. Add flour
and cook, stirring, for 1 minute,
then slowly add the fish stock and
cook, stirring, until thickened. Add
the lemon rind and juice, and
season with pepper.
3 Preheat the oven. Remove the
sauce from heat, stir in the cod,
mussels and parsley, then transfer to
an ovenproof dish. Mash the
potatoes with the remaining butter
and the milk. Season, then spread
evenly over the fish with a fork.
Cook in the oven for 30-40
minutes, until the sauce is bubbling
and the topping is starting to
brown.

Vegetable Dishes

Fresh vegetables are the dieter's closest companions, but without innovative ideas to vary their use they can elicit binge-producing boredom. So with a dash of innovation and a sprinkle of creativity we have compiled a collection of recipes to ensure that you will never look at onions, potatoes, peppers, and other gifts from the garden the same way again. Browse through the photographs on the following pages and you will see why wonderful things like frittatas, ratatouille, and puffs put a new twist on old favorites and ensure that vegetables will remain a welcome part of your daily dining.

Bubble and Squeak with Red Onion Chutney

Note: Originally a recipe to use up the leftovers from the Sunday roast, bubble and squeak is now found on the smartest restaurant menus. It's wonderful with the sweet chutney.

Serves 4
Preparation 25 mins
Cooking 30 mins
Calories 329
Fat 4g

1¹/₂ lb potatoes, peeled and cut into even-sized pieces
1 garlic clove, peeled
1 cup cabbage, finely shredded
4 spring onions, finely sliced
sea salt and freshly ground black pepper
2 tbsp butter
1 tbsp sunflower oil

Onion Chutney
2 large red onions, or 6 small red onions, finely chopped
4 tbsp golden sugar
1 tbsp white wine vinegar

1 Place the potatoes and garlic in a saucepan and cover with water. Bring to the boil, cover and simmer for 15–20 minutes, until tender. Drain, return to the pan, and mash until smooth. Cool.

2 Meanwhile, place the cabbage in a saucepan and pour over boiling water to just cover, bring back to the boil, then drain. Add the cabbage, spring onions, and seasoning to the potato and mix well.

3 Place all the ingredients for the chutney in a saucepan and bring to the boil over a low heat. Simmer gently, uncovered, for about 20 minutes or until almost all of the liquid has evaporated.

4 Divide the potato into eight and shape into flat rounds. Melt the butter and oil in a frying pan and fry cakes for 5 minutes on one side over a medium heat. Turn over, taking care as the cakes are quite soft, and cook for a further 5 minutes, until golden and heated through. Serve with chutney.

Pak Choi in Oyster Sauce

1 lb pak choi
3 tbsp oyster sauce
1 tbsp groundnut oil
salt

1 Trim the ends of the pak choi stalks, then separate the leaves and rinse thoroughly. Mix together the oyster sauce and oil.

2 Put the pak choi into a large saucepan of lightly salted boiling water and cook, uncovered, for 3 minutes or until tender. Drain thoroughly, return the pak choi to the pan, then add the oyster sauce and oil mixture and toss to coat evenly.

Note: Pak choi, the Chinese cabbage, should be cooked very quickly to retain its lovely crunchy texture. A generous dash of oyster sauce adds extra flavor to this dish.

Serves 4
Preparation 5 mins
Cooking 5 mins
Calories 64
Fat trace

Roasted Vegetables with Mozzarella

OVEN TEMPERATURE
450°F, 230°C, GAS 8

Serves 4
Preparation 25 mins
Cooking 35 mins
Calories 314
Fat 4.3g

2 carrots, cut into matchsticks
2 small waxy potatoes, sliced
salt and black pepper
olive oil for brushing
1 red and 1 green bell pepper,
each deseeded and cut into 8
pieces
1 eggplant, sliced
2 red onions, quartered
6 cloves garlic
1 ball mozzarella (about 5 oz),
grated

Sauce
1 tbsp olive oil
1 small onion, finely chopped
2 cloves garlic, crushed
2 cups canned chopped tomatoes
1 tbsp tomato purée
1 tsp dried oregano

1 Preheat the oven. Boil the carrots and potatoes in salted water for 2 minutes or until softened slightly, then drain.

2 To make the sauce, heat the oil in a heavy-based saucepan, and cook the onion and garlic over a low heat for 5 minutes or until softened. Add the tomatoes, tomato purée, and oregano. Bring to a boil, then reduce the heat and simmer, uncovered, for 20 minutes or until thickened.

3 Meanwhile, brush 2 large baking sheets with oil. Divide the carrots, potatoes, bell peppers, eggplant, onions, and garlic between the sheets, arranging in a single layer on each. Brush with oil, season, then roast for 20 minutes or until softened.

4 Spread the tomato sauce over the base of an ovenproof dish and arrange the vegetables on top. Sprinkle with mozzarella and return to the oven for 5 minutes or until the cheese has melted.

Chili Mushroom Stir-Fry with Noodles

½ oz dried porcini mushrooms
½ lb fresh Chinese noodles
2 tbsp sunflower oil
4 cloves garlic, sliced
1 red chili, deseeded
and chopped
2 tsp ready-made ginger purée
or finely grated ginger
1 lb mixed fresh mushrooms,
quartered
4 spring onions, sliced
4 tbsp sake or dry sherry
4 tbsp dark soy sauce
2 tbsp lemon juice
1 tbsp sugar, or to taste
2 tbsp chopped cilantro

1 Cover the dried mushrooms with 3 fl oz of boiling water and soak for 15 minutes or until softened. Strain and reserve the liquid, then slice the mushrooms. Meanwhile, prepare the noodles according to the packet instructions, until tender but still firm to the the bite, then drain.
2 Heat oil in a wok or large frying pan until smoking, then add garlic, chili, and ginger, and stir-fry for 15 seconds or until they release their flavors. Add all mushrooms, stir-fry for 2 minutes or until softened.
3 Add the spring onions, sake or sherry, soy sauce, lemon juice, sugar, cilantro, reserved soaking liquid from the mushrooms and the noodles, and heat for 1-2 minutes, until warmed through.

Note: The chili adds extra bite to this oriental mushroom and ginger stir-fry. Sake is Japanese rice wine; if you haven't got any you can use dry sherry instead.

Serves 4
Preparation 10 mins
plus 15 mins soaking
Cooking 10 mins
Calories 413
Fat 2.9g

Vegetable Tempura

Serves 4
Preparation 15 mins
Cooking 20 mins
Calories 286
Fat 1.1g

2 eggs
¹/₂ cup ice-cold water
¹/₂ cup plain flour, sieved
1 cup cranberry and orange
sauce, for dipping
vegetable oil, for deep-frying
1 zucchini, cut into thick slices
1 large red onion, cut into wedges
8 oz broccoli, cut into small
florets
1 red bell pepper, deseeded and
cut into strips
1 cup green beans, topped only
(not tailed)
1 cup asparagus, trimmed
sea salt
fresh basil leaves,
to garnish (optional)

1 To make batter, lightly whisk together eggs and water, then pour onto the flour all at once and whisk quickly, until the batter is smooth.
2 Heat cranberry and orange sauce in a small saucepan, over a gentle heat, until warm and runny. Remove from heat and place in a bowl.
3 Heat 2 inch of oil in a wok or frying pan. Dip the vegetables in to the batter and coat well. Test the temperature of the oil by dropping in a little batter, if it floats straight back to the surface the oil is hot enough.
4 Deep-fry the vegetables in small batches for 3–4 minutes or until crisp and golden. Remove with a slotted spoon and drain on kitchen paper. Season with salt. If using, deep-fry a few basil leaves for 20 seconds, until crisp. Serve the vegetables at once with the dipping sauce.

Root Vegetable Rösti

**2 potatoes, peeled and
coarsely grated**
1 parsnip, coarsely grated
1 carrot, coarsely grated
¹/₂ lb swede, coarsely grated
**1 tbsp butter, plus extra
for greasing**
1 tbsp sunflower oil
1 onion, chopped
**1 inch piece fresh
root ginger, peeled and grated**
1 medium egg, beaten
1 tbsp plain white flour
**sea salt and freshly ground
black pepper**
crispy bacon, to serve
fresh parsley, to garnish

1 Preheat the oven. Place the
grated potato, parsnip, carrot, and
swede in a clean tea towel and then
squeeze out any excess liquid. Heat
the butter and oil in a non-stick
frying pan. Fry the onion and
ginger for 5 minutes or until the
onion has softened.

2 Place the grated vegetables in a
large bowl, stir in onion and ginger
with the egg, flour and plenty of
seasoning. Mound the mixture on
to a greased baking sheet, to make a
8 inch round. Bake for 30–35
minutes, until golden and crispy at
the edges, and cooked through.
3 Carefully slide the vegetable rösti
onto a large serving plate. Add the
bacon (if using), garnish with fresh
parsley, and serve.

OVEN TEMPERATURE
375°F, 190°C, GAS 5

Serves 4
Preparation 25 mins
Cooking 40 mins
Calories 272
Fat 3.8g

Ratatouille in Fresh Tomato Sauce

Note: Fennel gives this quick vegetable dish a delicate aniseed flavor, while the sugar adds to the natural sweetness of the vegetables. Serve the ratatouille with long-grain rice.

Serves 4
Preparation 20 mins
Cooking 20 mins
Calories 193
Fat 1.4g

3 tbsp olive oil
2 cloves garlic, sliced
$1/4$ tsp chili flakes
2 red onions, sliced
1 eggplant,
cut into $1/2$ inch cubes
2 zucchini, cut into $1/2$ inch cubes
1 fennel bulb, cut into
$1/2$ inch cubes
1 yellow bell pepper, deseeded and
cut into $1/2$ inch cubes
6 plum tomatoes, chopped
juice of $1/2$ lemon
1 tbsp soft light or
dark brown sugar
1 tsp dried oregano
black pepper

1 Heat the oil in a large heavy-based saucepan, then add the garlic, chili flakes, if using, onions, eggplant, zucchini and fennel. Stir well, and cook, covered, for 10 minutes, stirring often, or until the vegetables have softened.
2 Add the yellow bell pepper, tomatoes, lemon juice, sugar, oregano, and seasoning to the onion mixture. Simmer, uncovered, for 10 minutes or until all the vegetables are tender, stirring occasionally.

Zucchini, Pepper, and Sweetcorn Frittata

2 tbsp olive oil
1 onion, chopped
2 cloves garlic, crushed
3 zucchini, sliced
1 red and 1 yellow bell pepper,
deseeded and sliced
$^1/_2$ cup canned sweetcorn,
drained
6 medium eggs
2 tbsp chopped fresh parsley
2 tbsp chopped fresh basil
$^1/_4$ tsp cayenne pepper
black pepper

1 Heat the oil in a large heavy-based frying pan with a flameproof handle. Add the onion, garlic, zucchini, and bell peppers, then fry for 10 minutes or until softened and golden. Stir in the sweetcorn.
2 Meanwhile, beat the eggs with the parsley, basil, cayenne pepper, and seasoning. Pour the mixture into the pan and cook over a low heat for 10 minutes or until the base is set and golden.
3 While the frittata is cooking, preheat the grill to medium. Place the pan under the grill and cook for 2-3 minutes until the top is golden brown and the frittata is cooked through.

Note: This omelette-style dish is filled with vegetables, so all you need to make a balanced meal is some crusty bread. Serve it hot or cold as part of a packed lunch or picnic.

Serves 4
Preparation 15 mins standing
Cooking 25 mins
Calories 254
Fat 3.3g

Stuffed Tomatoes with Chickpeas and Cilantro

Oven temperature
325°F, 160°C, Gas 3

Serves 4
Preparation 20 mins
Cooking 50 mins
Calories 148
Fat trace

2 slices day-old brown bread
4 large slicing tomatoes
1 clove garlic, crushed
¹/₂ cup canned chickpeas, drained
juice of 1 lemon
1 tbsp olive oil, plus extra
for greasing
1 red onion, finely chopped
¹/₄ tsp cayenne pepper
1 tsp ground cumin
1 tsp ground cilantro
4 tbsp chopped fresh cilantro
salt and black pepper

1 Preheat the oven. Place bread in oven for 20 minutes or until it becomes crisp. Process in a food processor to make breadcrumbs. Alternatively, use a grater. Increase oven temperature to 200°C/400°F/Gas Mark 6.

2 Slice off tomato tops and scoop out the insides. Place the shells upside-down on kitchen towels to drain. Put the insides and tops into a food processor with the garlic, chickpeas, and lemon juice and blend to a purée, or use a hand blender.

3 Heat the oil, then cook the onion with the cayenne pepper, cumin, and ground cilantro for 4-5 minutes, until softened. Mix with tomato mixture, breadcrumbs, fresh cilantro, and seasoning.

4 Spoon the mixture into the tomato shells. Place them on a lightly greased baking sheet and cook for 25 minutes, or until the tomatoes are tender.

Sun-Dried Tomato and Cheese Puffs

6 tbsp butter
1¹/₂ cups plain flour, sifted
¹/₂ tsp salt
4 medium eggs, beaten
1 cup Gruyère, grated

Stuffing
**¹/₃ cup sun-dried tomatoes in oil,
drained**
4 tbsp butter

Serves 16
Preparation 30 mins
plus 5 mins cooling
Cooking 30 mins
Calories 179 each
Fat 7g each

OVEN TEMPERATURE
425°F, 220°C, GAS 7

*Note: Gruyère
combines beautifully
with sun-dried
tomatoes in these
rich cheese puffs,
which can be served
at a drinks party or
as a starter with
some salad.*

1 Preheat the oven. Gently heat the butter and 8 fl oz of water in a large saucepan for 5 minutes, or until the butter has melted. Bring to the boil, then remove from the heat and stir in the flour and salt. Beat with a wooden spoon until mixture forms a smooth ball.
2 Gradually add the eggs, beating well, until the dough is shiny. Stir in Gruyère. Place balls of dough (about 2 tablespoons each) onto a baking sheet and cook for 20 minutes or until risen and browned. Turn off the oven. Cut a slit in the top of each puff to let the steam escape. Return puffs to the cooling oven for 5 minutes, then remove and cool for a further 5 minutes.
3 Meanwhile, make the stuffing. Place the tomatoes and butter in a food processor and blend to a paste. Divide the paste between the puffs, packing it in with a teaspoon.

Moroccan Potato and Lemon Casserole

OVEN TEMPERATURE
400°F, 200°C, GAS 6

Note: A couple of chilies and a few spices give this casserole of lemony potatoes its authentic Moroccan flavor. Serve it with a plain vegetable, such as green cabbage.

Serves 4
Preparation 20 mins
Cooking 45 mins
Calories 406
Fat 2.9g

3 tbsp olive oil
2 onions, sliced
3 cloves garlic, chopped
2 red chilies, finely chopped
1 tsp ground cumin
1 tsp ground cilantro
**2 lb waxy potatoes, cut into
¼ inch thick slices**
**grated rind of 1 lemon,
and juice of 1 or 2 lemons**
4 cups vegetable stock
salt and black pepper
**4 tbsp light soured cream
to serve**
**3 tbsp chopped
fresh parsley to garnish**

1 Preheat the oven. Heat the oil in a flameproof and ovenproof casserole dish. Add the onions, garlic, chilies, cumin, and cilantro, then gently fry for 1-2 minutes to release their flavors.

2 Stir in the potatoes, lemon rind, and juice to taste, then add the stock and seasoning. Bring to the boil, cover, cook in oven for 40 minutes or until vegetables are tender and the liquid has reduced slightly.

3 Transfer to plates and top each serving with a spoonful of soured cream. Sprinkle over fresh parsley to garnish.

Baked Onions with Mushrooms and Pine Nuts

2 slices brown bread
4 large Spanish onions
2 tbsp olive oil
2 cloves garlic, chopped
2 tbsp pine nut kernels
2 cups mushrooms, chopped
4 tbsp chopped fresh parsley
salt and black pepper

1 Preheat the oven. Place bread in the oven for 20 minutes or until it becomes crisp. Process in a food processor to make breadcrumbs.
2 Meanwhile, slice tops and bases off onions. Place in a saucepan, cover with water and bring to boil. Cook for 10 minutes to soften. Drain, leave to cool for 20 minutes.

3 Increase the oven to 400°F/200°C/Gas Mark 6. Cut out the middle of each onion, leaving the shell intact, and finely chop. Heat the oil, then fry the garlic and chopped onion for 5 minutes. Add the pine nuts and mushrooms and fry for a further 5 minutes. Remove from the heat, then mix in the breadcrumbs, parsley and seasoning. Fill the onion shells with the mixture, then wrap each onion in foil, leaving the tops open. Place on a baking sheet and cook for 40 minutes or until the onions are tender.

OVEN TEMPERATURE
325°F, 160°C, GAS 3

Serves 4
Preparation 20 mins
Cooking 40 mins plus
20 mins cooling
Calories 207
Fat 1.4g

Orange-Glazed Cabbage

OVEN TEMPERATURE
400°F, 200°C, GAS 6

Note: This unusual but very simple glaze of marmalade, orange juice, and maple syrup gives the cabbage a lovely sweetness. This dish is particularly good with sausages.

Serves 4
Preparation 10 mins
Cooking 25 mins
Calories 152
Fat 0.50g

1 white cabbage, thinly sliced

Glaze
juice of 2 oranges
2 tbsp maple syrup
1 tbsp olive oil
3 tbsp marmalade
1 tsp salt

1   Preheat the oven. To make the glaze, place the orange juice, syrup, oil and marmalade in a large bowl and stir. Season, add the cabbage and mix to coat thoroughly.

2   Remove the cabbage from the bowl, reserving the glaze, and spread out on a large baking tray. Pour over half of the reserved glaze and cook for 15 minutes. Remove from the oven, toss the cabbage gently, then pour over the rest of the glaze. Return to the oven and bake for a further 10 minutes or until the cabbage has turned dark brown at the edges.

Spicy Cauliflower with Garlic

2 slices brown bread
1 cauliflower, cut into florets
salt and black pepper
4 tbsp olive oil
1 clove garlic, crushed
1 red chili, finely chopped
8 black olives, pitted
and halved
1 tbsp capers

1 Preheat the oven. Place the bread in the oven for 20 minutes or until it dries out and becomes crisp. Process in a food processor to make breadcrumbs.

2 Place the cauliflower in a saucepan, cover with boiling water and add a little salt. Return to a boil, simmer for 1 minute or until slightly softened, then drain well.

3 Heat the oil in a large, heavy-based frying pan. Add the garlic, chili and cauliflower and fry for 3 minutes or until the cauliflower starts to brown. Add the olives, capers, breadcrumbs, and seasoning. Fry for a further 1 minute or until the breadcrumbs soak up the oil and flavorings.

OVEN TEMPERATURE
325°F, 160°C, GAS 3

Note: This method of cooking cauliflower comes from Italy. The fantastic combination of Mediterranean flavors will revolutionize your attitude towards this humble vegetable.

Serves 4   **Preparation** 10 mins   **Cooking** 25 mins   **Calories** 199   **Fat** 2g

Desserts and Baking

Tempt your taste buds and trim your waistline with our range of delicious desserts. Our luscious collection of after-dinner delights range from a humble fruit salad to mini chocolate muffins lashed with mocha sauce. Your mouth will water with each experience that will leave you wondering whether our recipes are truly low fat. Rest assured, we have struck the right balance between good health and great taste to bring you these sumptuous offerings, so prepare to be thrilled. Throw away your junk food and dodge the candy aisle at the supermarket because you are in for a real treat!

Oriental Fruit Salad

Note: If you're serving a very spicy or rich meal, give your guests this light and unusual fruit salad to finish. It will go with almost any meal — English, French, Thai...

Serves 4
Preparation 30 mins plus 20 mins cooling and 30 mins chilling
Cooking 5 mins
Calories 200
Fat trace

3 stalks lemon grass
¼ cup superfine sugar
1 small cantaloupe melon
1 mango
14 oz can lychees, drained
fresh mint leaves to garnish

1 Peel outer layers from lemon grass stalks, finely chop lower white bulbous parts, and discard the fibrous tops. Place lemon grass, sugar and 4 fl oz of water in a saucepan. Simmer, stirring, for 5 minutes or until sugar dissolves, then bring to a boil. Remove from heat and leave to cool for 20 minutes. Refrigerate for 30 minutes.

2 Halve the melon and scrape out the seeds. Cut into wedges, then remove skin and cut the flesh into small chunks. Slice off the two fat sides of mango close to the stone. Cut a criss-cross pattern across the flesh (but not the skin) of each piece, then push the skin inside out to expose the cubes of flesh and cut them off.
3 Place the melon, mango and lychees in serving bowls. Strain the lemon grass syrup and pour over the fruit. Decorate with mint.

Summer Pudding with Redcurrant Sauce

2 lb fresh or frozen mixed berry fruits
3 tbsp superfine sugar
8 slices white or wholemeal bread, crusts removed
2 tbsp redcurrant jelly

Serves 6
Preparation 10 mins plus 2-3 hrs chilling
Cooking 8 mins
Calories 177
Fat trace

Note: This is many people's favorite pudding – it's easy to make and healthy too. However, it just wouldn't taste the same without at least a spoonful of whipped cream.

1 Place the fruit, sugar and 3 tablespoons of water in a saucepan and simmer for 5 minutes or until the fruit has softened. Leave to cool slightly.

2 Line the base and sides of a 4 cup pudding basin with 6 slices of the bread, cutting to fit and making sure there are no gaps. Strain the fruit, reserving the juice, then add the fruit to the basin. Cover with the remaining bread to form a lid. Spoon over 3-4 tablespoons of the reserved juice.

3 Place a plate on top of the bread, with a weight, such as a large can, on it. Place in the fridge for 2-3 hours to let the juices soak through the bread.

4 For the sauce, strain the reserved juice into a pan, then add the redcurrant jelly. Simmer for 2-3 minutes, stirring, until the jelly has melted. Invert the pudding onto a plate and serve with the redcurrant sauce.

Strawberry Trifle Brulee

Serves 4
Preparation 15 mins
plus 2 hrs chilling
Cooking 3 mins
Calories 135
Fat 2.7g

**1 cup amaretti biscuits,
roughly crushed, or 2 trifle
sponges, cut in half
2 tbsp Madeira, sweet sherry
or kirsch
$^1/_2$ cup whipping or
light cream
4 cups ready-made custard
1 cup strawberries, hulled and
halved
3 tbsp demerara sugar**

1 Divide biscuits or sponge halves
between four 5 fl oz ramekins and
spoon over the Madeira, sherry, or
kirsch.
2 Whip the cream until it forms
soft peaks, then fold in the custard
and strawberries. Divide the cream
mixture between the ramekins.
Smooth the tops and sprinkle over a
thick layer of sugar.
3 Meanwhile, preheat the grill to
high. Place the ramekins under the
grill for 2-3 minutes, until the sugar
caramelizes. Leave to cool, then
refrigerate for 2 hours before
serving.

Plum Tart with Crumble Topping

**7 oz shortcrust pastry,
defrosted if frozen
1 lb plums or damsons, halved
and stoned
3 tbsp superfine sugar
1 tsp cornstarch
1/2 cup chopped mixed nuts
2 tbsp demerara sugar
2 tbsp fresh breadcrumbs**

1   Preheat the oven. Roll the pastry out thinly on a lightly floured surface and line a 8 in loose-bottomed flan tin. Refrigerate for ten minutes, then line with baking paper and baking beans. Cook for fifteen minutes, then remove the paper and beans and cook for another five minutes or until lightly golden. Cool for five minutes.

2   Meanwhile, put the plums or damsons into a saucepan with four tablespoons of water and the superfine sugar. Cook gently, covered, for 5 minutes or until the fruit is soft. Blend the cornstarch with 1 tablespoon of water. Stir into the fruit mixture and cook for 1 minute or until the juices thicken slightly.

3   Place plums, cut-side up, with any juices in the pastry case. Mix together nuts, demerara sugar and breadcrumbs and sprinkle over fruit. Bake 15 minutes or until topping is golden.

OVEN TEMPERATURE
325°F, 160°C, GAS 3

*Note: Served hot with lashings of custard, this pudding is perfect for a cold winter's night.
You can make it a day in advance and reheat it, but keep it in the fridge.*

Serves 6
Preparation 15 mins plus 10 mins chilling and 5 mins cooling
Cooking 35 mins
Calories 479
Fat 3.8g

Fresh Fruit Salad

Serves 4
Preparation 20 mins
plus 1 hr chilling
Calories 190
Fat trace

2 oranges
2-3 tbsp fresh, unsweetened orange juice
1 red eating apple, cored but not peeled, cut into $^1/_2$ inch pieces
1 pear, cored, peeled and cut into 1$^1/_2$ inch pieces
$^1/_2$ cup seedless grapes
1 ripe nectarine, skinned, stoned and cut into chunks
1 banana
6 fresh strawberries
non-fat yogurt

1 Slice the top and bottom off each orange and place on a work surface. Using a serrated knife, cut off the skin and pith, following the curves of the fruit. Holding the oranges over a bowl, cut between the membranes to release the segments. Put the segments into a large serving bowl with the orange juice.

2 Add the apple, pear, grapes, and nectarine to the bowl, and mix gently but thoroughly so that the orange juice coats the fruit (this will stop the fruit discoloring). Put the fruit salad in the fridge and chill for 1 hour to allow the flavors to develop.

3 Just before serving, peel the banana and slice thinly, then add to the bowl. Remove the green hulls from the strawberries, cut in half and add to the bowl. Mix gently and serve with non-fat yogurt.

Summer Fruit Compote
with Vanilla Yogurt

**1¹/₂ lb mixed summer berries,
hulled or stalks removed and
defrosted if frozen**
¹/₂ cup port
¹/₄ cup superfine sugar
2 strips orange rind
juice of 1 orange
1 tsp ground mixed spice

Vanilla Yogurt
1 vanilla pod, split
1 cup tub Greek yogurt
1 tbsp clear honey

1 To make the vanilla yogurt,
scrape the seeds from the vanilla
pod into the yogurt and stir in the
honey. Cover and refrigerate while
you make the compote.
2 Put the berries into a saucepan
with the port, sugar, orange rind
and juice, and the mixed spice.
Heat for 5-8 minutes, until fruit is
just softened. Remove from heat
and set aside for 15 minutes to cool
slightly. Serve the warm compote
with a spoonful of vanilla yogurt.

*Note: Thick vanilla
yogurt made with
clear honey has a
real Mediterranean
flavor, and tastes
fabulous with this
warm summer fruit
compote. Serve with
dessert biscuits.*

Serves 4
Preparation 30 mins
plus 15 mins cooling
Cooking 8 mins
Calories 202
Fat trace

Glossary

acidulated water: water with added acid, such as lemon juice or vinegar, which prevents discoloration of ingredients, particularly fruit or vegetables. The proportion of acid to water is 1 teaspoon per 300mL.

al dente: Italian cooking term for ingredients that are cooked until tender but still firm to the bite; usually applied to pasta.

americaine: method of serving seafood–usually lobster and monkfish–in a sauce flavored with olive oil, aromatic herbs, tomatoes, white wine, fish stock, brandy, and tarragon.

anglaise: cooking style for simple cooked dishes such as boiled vegetables. Assiette anglaise is a plate of cold cooked meats.

antipasto: Italian for "before the meal," it denotes an assortment of cold meats, vegetables, and cheeses, often marinated, served as an hors d'oeuvre. A typical antipasto might include salami, prosciutto, marinated artichoke hearts, anchovy fillets, olives, tuna fish, and Provolone cheese.

au gratin: food sprinkled with breadcrumbs, often covered with cheese sauce, and browned until a crisp coating forms.

balsamic vinegar: a mild, extremely fragrant, wine-based vinegar made in northern Italy. Traditionally, the vinegar is aged for at least seven years in a series of casks made of various woods.

baste: to moisten food while it is cooking by spooning or brushing on liquid or fat.

baine marie: a saucepan standing in a large pan, which is filled with boiling water to keep liquids at simmering point. A double boiler will do the same job.

beat: to stir thoroughly and vigorously.

beurre manie: equal quantities of butter and flour kneaded together and added a little at a time to thicken a stew or casserole.

bird: see paupiette.

blanc: a cooking liquid made by adding flour and lemon juice to water in order to keep certain vegetables from discoloring as they cook.

blanch: to plunge into boiling water and then, in some cases, into cold water. Fruits and nuts are blanched to remove skin easily.

blanquette: a white stew of lamb, veal, or chicken, bound with egg yolks and cream and accompanied by onion and mushrooms.

blend: to mix thoroughly.

bonne femme: dishes cooked in the traditional French "housewife" style. Chicken and pork bonne femme are garnished with bacon, potatoes, and baby onion; fish bonne femme with mushrooms in a white wine sauce.

bouquet garni: a bunch of herbs, usually consisting of sprigs of parsley, thyme, marjoram, rosemary, a bay leaf, peppercorns, and cloves, tied in muslin and used to flavor stews and casseroles.

braise: to cook whole or large pieces of poultry, game, fish, meat, or vegetables in a small amount of wine, stock, or other liquid in a closed pot. Often the main ingredient is first browned in fat and then cooked in a low oven or very slowly on top of the stove. Braising suits tough meats and older birds and produces a mellow, rich sauce.

broil: the American term for grilling food.

brown: cook in a small amount of fat until brown.

burghul (also bulgur): a type of cracked wheat, where the kernels are steamed and dried before being crushed.

buttered: to spread with softened or melted butter.

butterfly: to slit a piece of food in half horizontally, cutting it almost through so that when opened it resembles butterfly wings. Chops, large shrimp (prawns), and thick fish fillets are often butterflied so that they cook more quickly.

buttermilk: a tangy, low-fat cultured milk product whose slight acidity makes it an ideal marinade base for poultry.

calzone: a semicircular pocket of pizza dough, stuffed with meat or vegetables, sealed and baked.

caramelize: to melt sugar until it is a golden brown syrup.

champignons: small mushrooms, usually canned.

chasseur: (hunter) a French cooking style in which meat and chicken dishes are cooked with mushrooms, shallots, white wine, and often tomato.

clarify: to melt butter and drain the oil off the sediment.

coat: to cover with a thin layer of flour, sugar, nuts, crumbs, poppy or sesame seeds, cinnamon sugar, or a few of the ground spices.

concasser: to chop coarsely, usually tomatoes.

confit: from the French verb confire, meaning to preserve. Food that is made into a preserve by cooking very slowly and thoroughly until tender. In the case of meat, such as duck or goose, it is cooked in its own fat, and covered with it so that it does not come into contact with the air. Vegetables such as onions are good in confit.

consomme: a clear soup usually made from beef.

coulis: a thin puree, usually of fresh or cooked fruit or vegetables, which is soft enough to pour (couler means "to run"). A coulis may be rough-textured or very smooth.

court bouillon: the liquid in which fish, poultry, or meat is cooked. It usually consists of water with bay leaf, onion, carrots, and salt and freshly ground black pepper to taste. Other additives can include wine, vinegar, stock, garlic, or spring onions (scallions).

couscous: cereal processed from semolina into pellets, traditionally steamed and served with meat and vegetables in the classic North African stew of the same name.

cruciferous vegetables: certain members of the mustard, cabbage, and turnip families with cross-shaped flowers and strong aromas and flavors.

cream: to make soft, smooth, and creamy by rubbing with back of spoon or by beating with mixer. Usually applied to fat and sugar.

croutons: small toasted or fried cubes of bread.

crudites: raw vegetables, whether cut in slices or sticks to nibble plain or with a dipping sauce, or shredded and tossed as salad with a simple dressing.

cube: to cut into small pieces with six equal sides.

curdle: to cause milk or sauce to separate into solid and liquid. Example, overcooked egg mixtures.

daikon radish: (also called mooli) a long white Japanese radish.

Dark sesame oil: (also called Oriental sesame oil) dark polyunsaturated oil with a low burning point, used for seasoning. Do not replace with lighter sesame oil.

deglaze: to dissolve congealed cooking juices or glaze on the bottom of a pan by adding a liquid, then scraping and stirring vigorously while bringing the liquid to the boil. Juices may be used to make gravy or to add to sauce.

degrease: to skim grease from the surface of liquid. If possible the liquid should be chilled so the fat solidifies. If not, skim off most of the fat with a large metal spoon, then trail strips of paper towel on the surface of the liquid to remove any remaining globules.

devilled: a dish or sauce that is highly seasoned with a hot ingredient such as mustard, Worcestershire sauce or cayenne pepper.

dice: to cut into small cubes.

dietary fiber: a plant-cell material that is undigested or only partially digested in the human body, but which promotes healthy digestion of other food matter.

dissolve: mix a dry ingredient with liquid until absorbed.

dredge: to coat with a dry ingredient, as flour or sugar.

drizzle: to pour in a fine thread-like stream over a surface.

dust: to sprinkle or coat lightly with flour or icing sugar.

Dutch oven: a heavy casserole with a lid usually made from cast iron or pottery.

emulsion: a mixture of two liquids that are not mutually soluble– for example, oil and water.

entree: in Europe, the "entry" or hors d'oeuvre; in North America entree means the main course.

fillet: special cut of beef, lamb, pork, or veal; breast of poultry and game; fish cut of the bone lengthways.

flake: to break into small pieces with a fork.

flame: to ignite warmed alcohol over food.

fold in: a gentle, careful combining of a light or delicate mixture with a heavier mixture using a metal spoon.

fricassee: a dish in which poultry, fish, or vegetables are bound together with a white or veloute sauce. In Britain and the United States, the name applies to an old-fashioned dish of chicken in a creamy sauce.

galette: sweet or savoury mixture shaped as a flat round.

garnish: to decorate food, usually with something edible.

gastrique: caramelized sugar deglazed with vinegar and used in fruit-flavored savoury sauces, in such dishes as duck with orange.

glaze: a thin coating of beaten egg, syrup, or aspic which is brushed over pastry, fruits, or cooked meats.

gluten: a protein in flour that is developed when dough is kneaded, making it elastic.

gratin: a dish cooked in the oven or under the grill so that it develops a brown crust. Breadcrumbs or cheese may be sprinkled on top first. Shallow gratin dishes ensure a maximum area of crust.

grease: to rub or brush lightly with oil or fat.

joint: to cut poultry, game, or small animals into serving pieces by dividing at the joint.

julienne: to cut food into match-like strips.

knead: to work dough using heel of hand with a pressing motion, while stretching and folding the dough.

line: to cover the inside of a container with paper, to protect or aid in removing mixture.

infuse: to immerse herbs, spices, or other flavorings in hot liquid to flavor it. Infusion takes from two to five minutes, depending on the flavoring. The liquid should be very hot but not boiling.

jardiniere: a garnish of garden vegetables, typically carrots, pickling onions, French beans, and turnips.

lights: lungs of an animal, used in various meat preparations such as pâtes and faggots.

macerate: to soak food in liquid to soften.

marinade: a seasoned liquid, usually an oil and acid mixture, in which meats or other foods are soaked to soften and give more flavor.

marinara: Italian "sailor's style" cooking that does not apply to any particular combination of ingredients. Marinara tomato sauce for pasta is most familiar.

marinate: to let food stand in a marinade to season and tenderize.

mask: to cover cooked food with sauce.

melt: to heat until liquified.

mince: to grind into very small pieces.

mix: to combine ingredients by stirring.

monounsaturated fats: one of three types of fats found in foods. Are believed not to raise the level of cholesterol in the blood.

nicoise: a garnish of tomatoes, garlic, and black olives; a salad with anchovy, tuna and French beans is typical.

non-reactive pan: a cooking pan whose surface does not chemically react with food. Materials used include stainless steel, enamel, glass, and some alloys.

noisette: small "nut" of lamb cut from boned loin or rack that is rolled, tied, and cut in neat slices. Noisette also means flavored with hazelnuts, or butter cooked to a nut brown colour.

normande: a cooking style for fish, with a garnish of shrimp, mussels, and mushrooms in a white wine cream sauce; for poultry and meat, a sauce with cream, Calvados, and apple.

olive oil: various grades of oil extract from olives. Extra virgin olive oil has a full, fruity flavor and the lowest acidity. Virgin olive oil is slightly higher in acidity and lighter in flavor. Pure olive oil is a processed blend of olive oils and has the highest acidity and lightest taste.

panade: a mixture for binding stuffings and dumplings, notably quenelles, often of choux pastry or simply breadcrumbs. A panade may also be made of frangipane, pureed potatoes, or rice.

papillote: to cook food in oiled or buttered greasepoof paper or aluminium foil. Also a decorative frill to cover bone ends of chops and poultry drumsticks.

parboil: to boil or simmer until part cooked (i.e. cooked further than when blanching).

pare: to cut away outside covering.

pâte: a paste of meat or seafood used as a spread for toast or crackers.

paupiette: a thin slice of meat, poultry, or fish spread with a savoury stuffing and rolled. In the United States this is also called "bird" and in Britain an "olive."

peel: to strip away outside covering.

plump: to soak in liquid or moisten thoroughly until full and round.

poach: to simmer gently in enough hot liquid to cover, using care to retain shape of food.

polyunsaturated fat: one of the three types of fats found in food. These exist in large quantities in such vegetable oils as safflower, sunflower, corn, and soya bean. These fats lower the level of cholesterol in the blood.

puree: a smooth paste, usually of vegetables or fruits, made by putting foods through a sieve, food mill, or liquefying in a blender or food processor.

ragout: traditionally a well-seasoned, rich stew containing meat, vegetables, and wine. Nowadays, a term applied to any stewed mixture.

ramekins: small oval or round individual baking dishes.

reconstitute: to put moisture back into dehydrated foods by soaking in liquid.

reduce: to cook over a very high heat, uncovered, until the liquid is reduced by evaporation.

refresh: to cool hot food quickly, either under running water or by plunging it into iced water, to stop it cooking. Particularly for vegetables, and occasionally for shellfish.

rice vinegar: mild, fragrant vinegar that is less sweet than cider vinegar and not as harsh as distilled malt vinegar. Japanese rice vinegar is milder than the Chinese variety.

roulade: a piece of meat, usually pork or veal, that is spread with stuffing, rolled, and often braised or poached. A roulade may also be a sweet or savoury mixture that is baked in a Swiss roll tin or paper case, filled with a contrasting filling, and rolled.

rubbing-in: a method of incorporating fat into flour, by use of fingertips only. Also incorporates air into mixture.

safflower oil: the vegetable oil that contains the highest proportion of polyunsaturated fats.

salsa: a juice derived from the main ingredient being cooked or a sauce added to a dish to enhance its flavor. In Italy the term is often used for pasta sauces; in Mexico the name usually applies to uncooked sauces served as an accompaniment, especially to corn chips.

saturated fats: one of the three types of fats found in foods. These exist in large quantities in animal products, coconut, and palm oils; they raise the level of cholesterol in the blood. As high cholesterol levels may cause heart disease, saturated fat consumption is recommended to be less than 15% of calories provided by the daily diet.

sauté: to cook or brown in small amount of hot fat.

score: to mark food with cuts, notches of lines to prevent curling or to make food more attractive.

scald: to bring just to boiling point, usually for milk. Also to rinse with boiling water.

sear: to brown surface quickly over high heat in hot dish.

seasoned flour: flour with salt and pepper added.

sift: to shake a dry, powdered substance through a sieve or sifter to remove any lumps and give lightness.

simmer: to cook food gently in liquid that bubbles steadily just below boiling point so that the food cooks in even heat without breaking up.

singe: to quickly flame poultry to remove all traces of feathers after plucking.

skim: to remove a surface layer (often of impurities and scum) from a liquid with a metal spoon or small ladle.

slivered: sliced in long, thin pieces, usually refers to nuts, especially almonds.

soften: ie: gelatine. Sprinkle over cold water and allow to gel (soften) then dissolve and liquefy.

souse: to cover food, particularly fish, in wine vinegar and spices and cook slowly; the food is cooled in the same liquid. Sousing gives food a pickled flavor.

steep: to soak in warm or cold liquid in order to soften food and draw out strong flavors or impurities.

stir-fry: to cook thin slices of meat and vegetable over a high heat in a small amount of oil, stirring constantly to even cooking in a short time. Traditionally cooked in a wok, however a heavy based frying pan may be used.

stock: a liquid containing flavors, extracts, and nutrients of bones, meat, fish, or vegetables.

stud: to adorn with; for example, baked ham studded with whole cloves.

sugo: an Italian sauce made from the liquid or juice extracted from fruit or meat during cooking.

sweat: to cook sliced or chopped food, usually vegetables, in a little fat and no liquid over very low heat. Foil is pressed on top so that the food steams in its own juices, usually before being added to other dishes.

timbale: a creamy mixture of vegetables or meat baked in a mould. French for "kettledrum"; also denotes a drum-shaped baking dish.

thicken: to make a thin, smooth paste by mixing together arrowroot, corn flour, or flour with an equal amount of cold water; stir into hot liquid, cook, stirring until thickened.

toss: to gently mix ingredients with two forks or fork and spoon.

total fat: the individual daily intake of all three fats previously described in this glossary. Nutritionists recommend that fats provide no more than 35% of the energy in the diet.

vine leaves: tender, lightly flavored leaves of the grapevine, used in ethnic cuisine as wrappers for savoury mixtures. As the leaves are usually packed in brine, they should be well rinsed before use.

whip: to beat rapidly, incorporate air, and produce expansion.

zest: thin outer layer of citrus fruits containing the aromatic citrus oil. It is usually thinly pared with a vegetable peeler, or grated with a zester or grater to separate it from the bitter white pith underneath.

Weights & Measures

Cooking is not an exact science: one does not require finely calibrated scales, pipettes, and scientific equipment to cook, yet the conversion to metric measures in some countries and its interpretations must have intimidated many a good cook.

Weights are given in the recipes only for ingredients such as meats, fish, poultry, and some vegetables. Though a few grams/ounces one way or another will not affect the success of your dish.

Though recipes have been tested using the Australian Standard 250mL cup, 20mL tablespoon, and 5mL teaspoon, they will work just as well with the US and Canadian 8 fl oz cup, or the UK 300mL cup. We have used graduated cup measures in preference to tablespoon measures so that proportions are always the same. Where tablespoon measures have been given, these are not crucial measures, so using the smaller tablespoon of the US or UK will not affect the recipe's success. At least we all agree on the teaspoon size.

For breads, cakes, and pastries, the only area which might cause concern is where eggs are used, as proportions will then vary. If working with a 250mL or 300mL cup, use large eggs (65g/2^1/$_4$oz), adding a little more liquid to the recipe for 300mL cup measures if it seems necessary. Use the medium-sized eggs (55g/2oz) with 8 fl oz cup measure. A graduated set of measuring cups and spoons is recommended, the cups in particular for measuring dry ingredients. Remember to level such ingredients to ensure their accuracy.

English measures
All measurements are similar to Australian with two exceptions: the English cup measures 300mL/10^1/$_2$fl oz, whereas the Australian cup measure 250mL/8^3/$_4$fl oz. The English tablespoon (the Australian dessertspoon) measures 14.8mL/^{1}/$_2$fl oz against the Australian tablespoon of 20mL/^{3}/$_4$fl oz.

American measures
The American reputed pint is 16 fl oz, a quart is equal to 32 fl oz and the American gallon, 128 fl oz. The Imperial measurement is 20 fl oz to the pint, 40 fl oz a quart and 160 fl oz one gallon. The American tablespoon is equal to 14.8 mL/^{1}/$_2$fl oz, the teaspoon is 5 mL/^{1}/$_6$fl oz. The cup measure is 250 mL/8^3/$_4$fl oz, the same as Australia.

Dry measures
All the measures are level, so when you have filled a cup or spoon, level it off with the edge of a knife. The scale below is the "cook's equivalent"; it is not an exact conversion of metric to imperial measurement. To calculate the exact metric equivalent yourself, multiply ounces by 28.349523 to obtain grams, or divide 28.349523 grams to obtain ounces.

Metric	Imperial
g = grams	oz = ounces
kg = kilograms	lb = pound
15g	^{1}/$_2$ oz
20g	^{2}/$_3$ oz
30g	1 oz
55g	2 oz
85g	3 oz
115g	4 oz/^{1}/$_4$ lb
125g	4^1/$_2$ oz
140/145g	5 oz
170g	6 oz
200g	7 oz
225g	8 oz/^{1}/$_2$ lb
315g	11 oz
340g	12 oz/^{3}/$_4$ lb
370g	13 oz
400g	14 oz
425g	15 oz
455g	16 oz/1 lb
1,000g/1kg	35.3 oz/2.2 lb
1.5kg	3.3 lb

Oven temperatures
The Celsius temperatures given here are not exact; they have been rounded off and are given as a guide only. Follow the manufacturer's temperature guide, relating it to oven description given in the recipe. Remember gas ovens are hottest at the top, electric ovens at the bottom, and convection-fan forced ovens are usually even throughout. We included Regulo numbers for gas cookers which may assist.

To convert °C to °F, multiply °C by 9, and divide by 5, then add 32.

Oven temperatures

	C°	F°	Gas regulo
Very slow	120	250	1
Slow	150	300	2
Moderately slow	160	325	3
Moderate	180	350	4
Moderately hot	190-200	370-400	5-6
Hot	210-220	410-440	6-7
Very hot	230	450	8
Super hot	250-290	475-500	9-10

Cake dish sizes

metric	imperial
15 cm	6 in
18 cm	7 in
20 cm	8 in
23 cm	9 in

Loaf dish sizes

metric	imperial
23x12 cm	9x5 in
25x8 cm	10x3 in
28x18 cm	11x7 in

Liquid measures

metric	imperial	cup and spoon
mL	fl oz	
millilitres	fluid ounce	
5mL	$^1/_6$ fl oz	1 teaspoon
20mL	$^2/_3$ fl oz	1 tablespoon
30mL	1 fl oz	1 tablespoon plus 2 teaspoons
55mL	2 fl oz	$^1/_4$ cup
85mL	3 fl oz	
115mL	4 fl oz	$^1/_2$ cup
125mL	$4^1/_2$ fl oz	
150mL	$5^1/_4$ fl oz	
170mL	6 fl oz	$^3/_4$ cup
225mL	8 fl oz	1 cup
300mL	$10^1/_2$ fl oz	
370mL	13 fl oz	
400mL	14 fl oz	$1^3/_4$ cups
455mL	16 fl oz	2 cups
570mL	20 fl oz	$2^1/_2$ cups
1 litre	35.3 fl oz	4 cups

Cup measurements

One cup is equal to the following weights.

	Metric	Imperial
Almonds, flaked	85g	3 oz
Almonds, slivered, ground	125g	$4^1/_2$ oz
Almonds, kernel	155g	$5^1/_2$ oz
Apples, dried, chopped	125g	$4^1/_2$ oz

	Metric	Imperial
Apricots, dried, chopped	190g	$6^3/_4$ oz
Breadcrumbs, packet	125g	$4^1/_2$ oz
Breadcrumbs, soft	55g	2 oz
Cheese, grated	115g	4 oz
Choc bits	$155^1/_2$g	5 oz
Coconut, desiccated	90g	3 oz
Cornflakes	30g	1 oz
Currants	$155^1/_2$g	5 oz
Flour	115g	4 oz
Fruit, dried (mixed, sultanas etc)	170g	6 oz
Ginger, crystallized, glace	250g	8 oz
Honey, treacle, golden syrup	315g	11 oz
Mixed peel	225g	8 oz
Nuts, chopped	115g	4 oz
Prunes, chopped	225g	8 oz
Rice, cooked	155g	$5^1/_2$ oz
Rice, uncooked	225g	8 oz
Rolled oats	90g	3 oz
Sesame seeds	115g	4 oz
Shortening (butter, margarine)	225g	8 oz
Sugar, brown	155g	$5^1/_2$ oz
Sugar, granulated or caster	225g	8 oz
Sugar, sifted icing	155g	$5^1/_2$ oz
Wheatgerm	60g	2 oz

Length

Some of us still have trouble converting imperial length to metric. In this scale, measures have been rounded off to the easiest-to-use and most acceptable figures. To obtain the exact metric equivalent in converting inches to centimeters, multiply inches by 2.54 whereby 1 inch equals 25.4 millimeters and 1 millimeter equals 0.03937 inches.

Metric	Imperial
mm=millimetres	in = inches
cm=centimetres	ft = feet
5 mm, 0.5 cm	$^1/_4$ in
10 mm, 1.0 cm	$^1/_2$ in
20 mm, 2.0 cm	$^3/_4$ in
2.5 cm	1 in
5 cm	2 in
$7^1/_2$ cm	3 in
10 cm	4 in
$12^1/_2$ cm	5 in
15 cm	6 in
18 cm	7 in
20 cm	8 in
23 cm	9 in
25 cm	10 in
28 cm	11 in
30 cm	12 in, 1ft

Index